CW01368866

NOW DEPARTING

NOW DEPARTING

A Small-Town Mortician on Death, Life,
and the Moments in Between

VICTOR M. SWEENEY

G

Gallery Books

New York   Amsterdam/Antwerp   London
Toronto   Sydney/Melbourne   New Delhi

G
Gallery Books
An Imprint of Simon & Schuster, LLC
1230 Avenue of the Americas
New York, NY 10020

For more than 100 years, Simon & Schuster has championed authors and the stories they create. By respecting the copyright of an author's intellectual property, you enable Simon & Schuster and the author to continue publishing exceptional books for years to come. We thank you for supporting the author's copyright by purchasing an authorized edition of this book.

No amount of this book may be reproduced or stored in any format, nor may it be uploaded to any website, database, language-learning model, or other repository, retrieval, or artificial intelligence system without express permission. All rights reserved. Inquiries may be directed to Simon & Schuster, 1230 Avenue of the Americas, New York, NY 10020 or permissions@simonandschuster.com.

Copyright © 2025 by Victor Sweeney

All rights reserved, including the right to reproduce this book or portions thereof in any form whatsoever. For information, address Gallery Books Subsidiary Rights Department, 1230 Avenue of the Americas, New York, NY 10020.

First Gallery Books hardcover edition October 2025

GALLERY BOOKS and colophon are registered trademarks of Simon & Schuster, LLC

Simon & Schuster strongly believes in freedom of expression and stands against censorship in all its forms. For more information, visit BooksBelong.com.

For information about special discounts for bulk purchases, please contact Simon & Schuster Special Sales at 1-866-506-1949 or business@simonandschuster.com.

The Simon & Schuster Speakers Bureau can bring authors to your live event. For more information or to book an event, contact the Simon & Schuster Speakers Bureau at 1-866-248-3049 or visit our website at www.simonspeakers.com.

Interior design by Hope Herr-Cardillo

Manufactured in the United States of America

10 9 8 7 6 5 4 3 2 1

Library of Congress Cataloging-in-Publication Data has been applied for.

ISBN 978-1-6680-6211-1
ISBN 978-1-6680-6213-5 (ebook)

To John, whom I love as a friend
And Alex, whom I loved as a brother
To Mike, my companion in Life and in Death

And to Paige, whom I love like no other

CONTENTS

Author's Note ix
Preface xi
1. The Sign of 1,600 Souls 1
2. A Good Funeral 11
3. Autumn in Namibia 25
4. A Farmer's Death 35
5. Walls of Conviction 49
6. Getting Lost 63
7. Death at the Rumor Mill 69
8. Grim Housekeeping 81
9. Night Call 87
10. And a Time to Laugh 103
11. A Banana or a Cup of Coffee 109
12. Why Not a Bone Ark? 119
13. Dying Away from Home 133
14. Waiting 141
15. The Mort-Wife 149
16. Knowledge at Your Fingertips 155
17. An Obituary 159
18. A Request 173

CONTENTS

19. The Usual Attire	179
20. Reckless Charity	185
21. Strictly Business	193
22. The Price We Pay for Love	199
23. In Living Memory	213
24. Open to Life, Open to Death	221
25. An Epitaph	231
26. The Curse	245
27. Friends Among the Living and the Dead	251
Afterword	269
Acknowledgments	271

AUTHOR'S NOTE

WE MUST REMEMBER OUR DEAD and get to know the living. To that effect, the stories in this book include the deaths and lives of the many I've met in my line of work. A few names and details have been changed to provide anonymity where requested. Outside of these select instances, my townspeople have trusted me to use their real names (and those of their loved ones who have departed) and tell their stories alongside my own. I admit to seeing their lives and deaths through my own eyes, and as such, I might have missed things worth sharing while misremembering less-important facts along the way. Such is the fickleness of memory. But the act of remembering is a gift all the same and one I'm honored to share.

PREFACE

I WASN'T RAISED IN THE countryside, but that is where I find myself these days. It is also the place in which I wear many hats—ad hoc grave digger, obituary draftsman, liturgy organizer, headstone designer, community death mentor. Most of these fit comfortably enough when working in deathcare in a small town.

As a "country" mortician (funeral director, or the more archaic undertaker), I believe contentment is a choice, a purposeful culturing of active contentment inside oneself. Being happy with what I've got right now is easy, as I have all the things I need and some of the things I want. In a roundabout way, in 2021 I was thrust into the spotlight following a series of viral YouTube videos in which I answered questions about my career (more on that later), and some windows of opportunity seemed to open up to take me out of the rather quiet life I had. Some suggested there was more potential for me to tap into in the age of videos, views, and clicks. All sorts of producers came out of the woodwork after that, offering ways to get more out of my brief flash of micro-celebrity. One memorable individual pitched a death-related reality TV show in which contestants would reconstruct bodies and do makeup on the deceased—and I could be the host and judge!

Needless to say, this suggestion (and all others) wasn't that attractive when compared with the day-to-day work of making a difference in my neighbors' lives, and deaths, in this small corner of the world.

It wasn't lost on me, however, that I might have something to offer a larger community handling death in their own lives or those left pondering the fate that awaits us at the end of our days. It seemed possible that I could share thoughts and stories that have inspired me in my work and have helped me view the world in a way that accepts reality, strives for the good, and lets me sleep well at night after long days of handling dead bodies.

And so came about this book.

It is neither reality TV nor a pithy Q&A video series, but it is something closer to the way I think day in and day out. Throughout these pages, there are, I hope, moments of levity and moments that make one pause. These narratives stand alongside the practical truths of death, not only in a small town but everywhere—the physical meeting the metaphysical. Bodies and souls collide in life and separate in death—those of us who get too close to either are given a privileged view of what death means and a view of how to live. It is this very thing that I hope to share with you here.

Let it be so.
+Victor

NOW DEPARTING

1

THE SIGN OF 1,600 SOULS

"VICTOR, WE'LL BE BRINGING HER in shortly."

It's not every day the deceased is brought to the funeral home for me. As the local undertaker, I typically head to the place of death to retrieve the recently departed.

Even less common is that Dolores's husband and son want to bring her through the funeral home's garage and escort her into the embalming room themselves. In Minnesota, one can't enter a "prep room" without a license to practice mortuary science. This would be totally forbidden under any other circumstance. I know it. But I also know Chuck and Mike DuBore (husband and son, respectively) very well, so I don't put up any objections.

Not only will these two wheel their own cot with the departed on it into the embalming room, I know they'll lift her to the porcelain embalming table, remove her hospital gown, cover her with a sheet tucked up to her chin, and leave Dolores there for me.

They can do this and I let them, gladly.

Dolores is their wife and mother.

And they also own the funeral home.

I'll be embalming my boss Mike's mother. And my aging mentor, Chuck, will closely scrutinize the work on his wife when I'm done, he himself having embalmed innumerable bodies as Minnesota's oldest licensed mortician.

The "magic" of embalming will be lost on my customers today, the two of them being intimately familiar with the minutiae of how a body is prepared, knowing what to expect when they see Dolores, and trusting me to do something they could do themselves. But by allowing me to handle this, they are allowing me to return to them a gift. The work itself is strangely intimate, and I'd rather spare Mike the trouble of seeing his mother's lifeblood leave her body. As the matriarch of an undertaking family, Dolores knew our profession keenly, having watched her husband and son run from the house, night or day, to lay her neighbors to rest. That she has now become part of what they have given families, a returning of a favor of a sort is appropriate. She will become for them what her son and husband have sought to give others.

It's rare these days for me to get nervous when embalming. Having handled a few thousand bodies up to this point, dead humans don't offer much in the way of fear. Embalming is somewhere between art and science. Half of my chosen profession is unseen. Embalming happens behind closed and locked doors. It remains unknown to those outside the locked doors exactly how their loved ones are meticulously posed, preserved, and painted to give them a look of peacefulness, blissfully unaware of the somewhat grim realities that turn decomposing human flesh into what will become a representation of their loved one, returned to them for a final goodbye.

Dolores, of course, is an exception.

An initial inspection shows that she's lost more weight since last I saw her smiling at me out the passenger seat of Chuck's Buick Enclave while they were on their way to a restaurant the next town over. Dementia has brought struggles the last few years. First overeating, then undereating, with husband and son doing their best to alternately hide food and later push it. Chuck has been a model in patience, probably hard-won from years as the only funeral director in Warren, Minnesota. When you've worked with nearly every family in town over a career spanning six decades, you learn to be patient with what life brings.

On the table Dolores is thin. Her slender hands will be bedecked with rings when it comes time to dress her, and I'm told that Chuck will bring her rosary. In Catholic custom, the crucifix on the circlet of beads is held between the thumb and forefinger and draped around the hands, which will rest over the abdomen. When I'm done, her hands should look as if they are resting easy after a lifetime of work. Dolores delivered many babies with these two hands, working at our small hospital, and it isn't lost on anyone that she worked in the Comings of life while her husband worked in the Goings.

My career in the Goings of Warren is just over one decade old. About a third of my life, yet it seems to pale in comparison to Mike's thirty-plus years of experience and his dad Chuck's, which round out an even century of funeral service. When I first moved here, Mike's hair was still brown and his face free of wrinkles. While he works out every day to keep on top of a physically demanding job, Mike and I both watch each other age a little more as funerals mark the weeks, months, and years. Chuck seems ageless at eighty-eight, but of course he's not. Time continues to march on despite his timelessness, and I know the town itself continues to change, expanding and contracting almost daily. The contraction in population is marked by the uncontracting chests and the silent hearts that pass through my door, and the expansion by young couples willing to roll the dice and bring another child up in a town that is, to appearances, stuck in the 1950s.

Warren is a town of 1,600 people. There's a sign on State Highway 1 NW that tells passersby this fact. Little else but open fields greet the person driving through our tiny hamlet. The long space is finally broken by the cluster of trees that surround the Snake River and have thankfully grown thick enough through the city limits to block the prairie winds that blow the snow for just shy of half the year up here.

These are things I didn't know upon my arrival for a job interview. I saw the trees, but didn't know they bordered a muddy and often stagnant river. I saw the population sign and wondered at its smallness. The town's motto presciently proclaims this blip on the map as "Your New Hometown." This has come to pass. Having no knowledge of the people who inhabited the place or any idea what was in store for me, the Sign of 1,600 Souls did not impress upon me then, as it does now, the profound gratitude this small place on earth has afforded me.

When one of those souls goes, I get to go along with it, or

what remains of it, for at least part of its final journey, one that almost invariably starts with a phone call to the funeral home.

Will they be the parent of a friend, a neighbor, or someone known only in passing? Will my throat close when I hear their name, or will I be relieved that someone has died who was gladly awaiting it? "It was a blessing," we'll say.

I have no control over who it is or when it comes. I can only do what comes next, arriving to bring a body into my care.

I've pulled bodies from all sorts of places. Many come from hospitals or nursing homes. Others are brought from houses that range anywhere from squalid to prim. One woman had tucked herself in bed so perfectly that the sheets were crisp to the touch, her passing in the night leaving her body behind as the only evidence that something dramatic had happened. As an opposite sort of example, I cannot forget moving a half-naked gentleman who had been dead for some days into a body bag, rolling him over in the process and finding fifty-seven cents in change and a flip-flop stuck into the fat of his very purple back. You simply never know what awaits you on a death call.

One thing I find both in lived experience and in the profession at large is a dichotomy in search of a balance. One gets the good and the bad, the lovely and the unsettling, and the poignant with the mundane. Walking the world between the living and the dead, you get both sides of everything—and they tend to run closely together. It's part of the job to find the balance between the tension and to be a sort of guide for those on either side of this narrow chasm. My whole profession is a mash-up of a series of two wildly different things, each of them visible and both beautiful and ugly at once.

And today I will have to do something ugly in order to give something beautiful: the gift of having a wife and mother back, if only for a time.

Dolores will have her funeral in a handful of days. As I work with her on the table, posing facial features, swapping blood for preservative, and filling out some of the hollowness that her face has acquired over the last few weeks, attention to detail is heightened. Sometimes work is just work. But sometimes it is uniquely, oddly, and beautifully personal. Chuck took me aside before he departed from the funeral home to encourage me and asked that I be sure to fill her temples a little. Fit and upright as always, he has looked upon the diminishing body of his wife as a husband of nearly sixty years, but also as one who knows what ought to be done to make her look as she used to in better times than these.

When I am satisfied with her expression, her hands get posed just so. I'll give her fingernails a few coats of polish and her hair will have my closest supervision when the salon owner comes to fix it.

Mike and I get her dressed, and after that, his mother becomes visible again, looking more like "herself." Chuck has refrained from popping back in to check on us, as he usually does. He wants to wait until she's fully ready: dressed, casketed, hair done, and makeup applied.

The following morning, I'm at my desk working on the details of another funeral (death waits not even for the funeral home owner's grief) when Chuck passes the building, parks his truck, and lets himself into the chapel to see Dolores. He stays in there quietly for some time.

I hear the chapel doors close. He walks into my office and shakes my hand. Then we exchange a rare hug, and he slips me $100 in cash. There are no words spoken. His gratitude shows on his face.

After all is is prepared in advance of the funeral, the day finally comes, bringing with it Mike's family and friends and, oddly enough, several other morticians who have sprung up from this unlikely town in the middle of nowhere. Together, there are five of us licensees in attendance to lay the matriarch to rest. Even the priest was a licensed mortician before he took the collar. We do it with wan smiles, for there are worse things than death and we can be both happy and sad at the same time. As the Funeral Mass begins, I am in the back, watching over the proceedings, checking to be sure the lunch is getting situated in the social hall and all is as it should be with the church ladies before I confirm things at the cemetery. As I drive out to check that the grave digger and vault company are ready for our arrival within the next hour, my mind meanders for a moment.

I am struck with the thought of the Sign of 1,600 Souls. I know it ought now read 1,599. But only for a short while. Hope and gratitude are abundant enough that some foolish Warrenites will surely follow their instincts, begetting a child that will enter our community and start the cycle of the Comings and Goings anew.

As odd or unexpected as it may seem, those of us who get to walk where I do daily see life a little more brightly. Death colors our imaginations and they take flight. Approach a place where life and death intersect and you can instinctively feel the connection. A hospital, a nursing home. A cemetery is my preference.

My house sits one block away from Greenwood Cemetery. The other cemetery within the city limits is Calvary Catholic Cemetery, situated across the street from Greenwood, and in which Dolores now rests. The parklike aspect of either is attractive. My family and I often end up walking to the actual park through one or the other, but sometimes we don't get that far. Greenwood Cemetery is an especially easy place to play hide-and-seek, with the kids crouching behind the larger stones, being given away by their usual giggles. We've also found it a great place to learn to ride a bike. The roads are gravel and less suitable for bike riding, but there are rarely cars. It seems a shame to have it so unpopulated by the living, but on the other hand, we don't have to dodge traffic when little feet still haven't mastered the brakes. There's even a raised sort of mall in the middle where the veterans' display is, an elevated lawn ringed by massive landscaping blocks. We affectionately call it "the castle." This is where the children go to practice their balance, walking from brick to brick, fending off imaginary enemies hiding just behind a nearby headstone.

To me, a cemetery is where the dead and the living intersect, not only physically but on some other plane, too. It is a place of some preternatural tension, but not of a bad sort. Our loved ones are underfoot and yet my children still frolic and stomp barefoot through the dandelions growing above them. Most are buried shoeless, as well. The living go on and the dead remain. It is somehow so natural.

Before we depart from the cemetery on this frigid January day, I notice Dolores's casket is facing "backward" on the grave, with her feet to the west and not pointing east (toward the direction of the Resurrection), as is customary. All of us morticians shivering at the graveside grasp this gaffe simultaneously and shake our heads for not catching it right away. As the one in charge today, the blame falls on me, but I've been lost in thought, grieving and thinking about Mike and Chuck and their family.

THIS IS THE NATURE OF my time walking between the living and the dead. And as I am not yet the latter, I appreciate so much the great gift of the former.

After her family, my employer, and the other morticians depart, I rotate Dolores's casket into the proper position, the remaining witness as she's lowered into the frost-covered ground.

We, here, get to say our goodbyes today, and we will still say hello in some way tomorrow.

Hello.

From one of us as yet among the living.

2

A GOOD FUNERAL

THE BODY OF THE DEAD and its state are the two most immediate and emotion-provoking responsibilities we assume as morticians, and it's why so much of our craft is devoted to them. These are the last glimpses of physical recognition and connection we'll ever have with those who've been at the center of our lives. If Aunt Ginny has lost so much weight in the last months of her life and is an emaciated shadow of her former self, that unrecognizability in her body can be tough. We don't quite know what to do with ourselves (or our loved ones) when they don't look "right." How can we say goodbye to someone who isn't quite themself?

This is particularly challenging given that any inanimate body is not "right." To see a body lying perfectly still, immovable with no rising and falling of the chest, no flush to the cheeks or micro-twitching around the eyes—it's all uncanny and catches us off guard.

Our natural state is to have an animated body. Without that animating principle (whether we call it a soul or something else), the dead seem much more like terribly familiar objects than they do our once-living, once-breathing, once-moving loved ones.

We try to make the familiar as familiar as we can.

———•———

A DEATH CALL COMES LATE in the evening, as many do, it seems. I go to the hospital, retrieve a gentleman, arrive back at the funeral home as the moon rises, and proceed to embalm him for his funeral, to be held in the coming days. As I finish the very routine embalming, somewhat on autopilot, I'll admit, I stop and catch my breath:

Frenchie has always had a mustache . . . and he doesn't have one now.

I had seemingly committed one of the graver crimes an embalmer can perpetrate: I shaved off a mustache. Was I really that out of it? Panicking for a moment and letting my breathing return somewhat to normal, I call his wife. After apologizing for the lateness of the hour (no matter, Susan was awake anyway), I ask the question to which I dread the answer.

"Did Frenchie have a mustache?"

A pause.

One that lasts about 3.5 hours by my reckoning.

"No. Funny you should ask. A nurse shaved it off last week when he was in the hospital."

(I breathe a sigh of relief and my heart rises back into my chest out of my stomach.) But Susan has a question.

"Is there anything you can do about that, Victor?"

"Well, I can take a little hair from the back of his head and reconstruct one with wax, hair, and some effort, but it won't be perfect."

"Aw, Victor, never mind. You know, the last time I saw Frenchie clean-shaven was on our wedding day and that was fifty years ago; his mother insisted on it. I suppose if he's going to meet her, she'll be happy for that, anyway."

Cut to the day of the funeral.

It is all anybody is talking about. How Frenchie looks so much like his brother now that his mustache is missing, how Frenchie has cleaned up nice for the first time ever, how they hardly recognize him, except that his name is on the memorial card in their hand, et cetera. Even his family, who was prepared for this, think it odd to see Dad not looking "like himself." Afterward, a son tells me it all went well . . . except for the fact that it didn't seem like his dad in the casket and, later, in the ground.

And all of this over a mustache. As you can imagine, morticians deal with far worse changes or degradations to bodies than missing facial hair.

———•———

MY FIRST MORTICIAN BOSS, AT Korsmo Funeral Service in Moorhead, Minnesota, was a second-generation funeral director. His dad, Paul (ninety years old at the time), used to come in and putter around the funeral home, sometimes hanging out in the office, sometimes checking in on us in the dressing room (for the dead) after an embalming. He had a lot of aphorisms he shared in his Norwegian brogue, but the best one, the one that I still think about regularly because it seems stubbornly true no matter what else I do, is this:

You can't have a good funeral with a bad body.

If a body is so mangled it requires a closed casket, when the family might have otherwise had it open, it changes the nature of the funeral. It becomes an immensely harder thing. By not being able to see their loved one, a barrier is thrown up at a time when we want these loved ones close.

We morticians bear witness to the sometimes awful truth: the bones sticking out in places they ought not, or the slow wasting away that happens with cancer, or the plain fact of aging. Barriers like these and the pain of them is something embalmers try to help a family overcome.

The aphorism about preferring a "Good Body" to a "Bad Body" deals with the fact that we have a job to do in making folks presentable for viewing—and if we do a poor job, the rest of the service provided suffers. Our services begin at the time of the initial death call, but they hang in the balance on how we prepare the body, if we're called to do so. The preparation of the body includes: washing and embalming, as well as positioning (during the process and later in the casket), dressing, and putting on any makeup that's needed (given the spiffy name "cosmetizing" in the mortuary world). These will be the first things that families see and that attendees will notice, consciously or otherwise. If a modest maiden aunt's cosmetics are done to a stage-makeup level, we've got a problem. Or if Dad's lower lip is unembalmed, breaking down with skin sloughing off as we stand around the casket, there are issues present that will affect the rest of our day.

Of all these tasks, embalming may be the foundation on which the entire success of a presentation rests. It's not always required—you can lay out unembalmed bodies in quick scenarios generally involving cremation or immediate burial. But when faced with time between death and viewing, while that very same time is disintegrating a dead body, well, embalming is your friend.

Embalming is an interesting subject. It's equal parts science and art, beauty and grimness, creation and corruption. It follows the rest of the human condition in that respect. It's one of the many places in my world in which the good and the bad run side by side, hand in hand. Embalming isn't exactly glamorous in process, but the result is to try to make something that achieves a bit of magic.

One of the goals of embalming is to sanitize the body inside and out. It is important to start, however, outside-in. Everybody will get a wash with germicidal soap and a scrub with a sponge or brush, whether they look clean or are decidedly dirty. Hair will get a wash with some light shampoo; disinfectant will be sprayed beneath each eyelid, in mouths, and up each nostril. Bacteria love to grow in warm, wet cavities unprotected by immune systems, and a dead human face unfortunately fits the bill. After these quick but important steps in cleanliness are taken, everyone receives a face shave to one degree or another.

Now, this might seem off. For instance, my grandma MeMe doesn't shave. But when it comes to being dead—and lying very still—something like stray hairs or a large whisker on a chin becomes wildly noticeable. Were MeMe in the casket, her movements wouldn't distract me from her mustache the way they normally do. She also gets a trim, because if we put on any makeup, let's say over a small bruise or a postmortem dry spot, the mortuary cosmetics will stick to that hair and, again, really stand out. We want Grandma to be fully seen, not simply the fine and fuzzy beard that has grown unchecked during her last weeks in hospice.

Once a body is cleaned and shaved, it is time to "set the features." This is the process by which we arrange the facial features to look "peaceful." This part could also take longer than the active embalming, requiring what seems like an hour on the mouth and eyes during two hours in the prep room. Sometimes it is quick, sometimes painstaking. It varies as much as the person. As one of the most important components of mortuary art, we cannot neglect or rush it. The "peaceful look," that undefinable thing a mortician learns in his study of the living, should make the faces of our dead appear comforting rather than garish.

When I'm setting features, here's what I'm thinking about—a few tricks of the trade, if one can appreciate the art. The next time you're at a wake or funeral, this might be an interesting set of rarely discussed insights to observe and ponder as the ritual plays out around you.

First, some DON'Ts:

I don't like to use mouth formers—these are plastic teeth-cover things that purport to "give the mouth a natural shape," but in reality make a person look as if they're either wearing a mouthguard or packing a large dip of chewing tobacco. I like to use cotton to fill in any areas of the mouth that are sunken due to weight loss, missing dentures, et cetera. Cotton is easier to manipulate; it can be customized to the embalmer's heart's content.

Meanwhile, eyelids are also tricky—and the big thing here is you don't want to let them overlap. Eyelids should simply abut. Also note that your eyelids and mine don't rest exactly at the halfway point of the eye. This is reserved for a "pained grimace" expression. When sleeping, say, our eyelids rest along the lower third of the eye. To that point, getting lids to stay down sometimes requires assistance. An "eye cap" is like a burred contact lens, the little hooks keeping stubborn eyelids in place. Often with the elderly (and their thin skin), a small piece of cotton, spread sparingly, provides enough friction to prevent any "peeping."

And once more back to the mouth—don't leave it open. This was a thing embalmers used to do a generation ago to give a "natural, rested look." The jaw was slightly slackened, with the resulting gap between the lips filled in with mortuary wax after the fact. Don't do it. Just don't. Wax doesn't look natural, nor does the resulting long face.

And now some DOs:

When it comes to the mouth, each person's facial structure is different. If someone has dentures, odds are good their upper and lower jaws have less bone to work with. A big needle injector (a device that punches metal brads attached to wires into the bone to more easily tie them closed) will be too powerful and break the bone or have little purchase, with the brads falling out. Suturing through the lower frenulum (behind the lip) can work well, but can sometimes pull the mouth into a pout that looks puffy. You can also internally loop the lower jaw and tie it tight that way. I've also tied tooth to tooth or gone through the lingual (tongue) frenulum. Folks who advocate for a rolled towel or some such thing beneath the chin have never tried to keep it in place while vigorously manipulating the arms and legs to promote distribution and blood flow. Also, that towel will be absolutely sopping with blood by the end.

Finally, never forget to take your good, sweet time. I like to set up the mouth first before closing the eyes. Then I can test the shape of the mouth and the curve of a small smile while the eyes are open. It looks more natural to me. When I have it right, often adding just a bit of cotton under the orbicularis oris at the corner of the mouth to give the smile a slight upward tilt, I'll close the eyes.

I HAVE THIS IDEA THAT people who look most like "themselves" in the casket are those same people who lived their lives unashamedly. They were true to themselves, in both public and private, and so are recognizable when we see them laid out. For instance, the woman who had no qualms with her wrinkles and crow's-feet will look like "herself"; we don't have to painstakingly hide the effects of age on a woman who was never afraid of it. Or the gentleman who always wore bib overalls? We'll get him in his denims, mildly trim his beard, and find that he's recognizable; less so if he's in a suit. There's also a truth in the warning your mother gave you about making a face that will stay that way. The way we smile in life seems to fall into place naturally when we die. And conversely, frowners keep their grimace in death. But either one is recognizable. If Aunt Ginny frowned most of her days and only smiled when out in public, the frown is what will stick. I don't make any judgments here, but there's something to being who you are all the time. There are no secrets in death.

BUT, OF COURSE, THERE ARE times when, due to injury or things well outside anyone's control, a viewing cannot happen. A smile or a frown pales in comparison to the larger injuries sustained. But every so often, even the seemingly worst cases turn out okay. One case comes to mind in which I was able to see firsthand how patience and the right skill set could bring a loved one back for a time and the value that flowed from it.

We heard the fire trucks go out that evening as the kids got ready for bed. The station is across town from my house, but that only accounts for a handful of blocks. Around here, a siren usually means a car crash, as other types of major fires are blessedly rare. I always get a little expectant when I hear the sirens, though. It might mean nothing. It also might mean the start of some very hard days.

The next day, I hear through the grapevine that Jason Johnston was killed. He's a young guy, maybe forty. He's got a few kids, and his mother, Carey, usually waits on me at the bank when I deposit the paycheck that allows us to live in frugal comfort. As we hear the rumor that he was ejected through the windshield of his car, his mother calls.

Carey is emotionally wrought, and rightly so, but still wants to come in right away. I don't even have Jason's body yet. He'll be going to the medical examiner for an autopsy (due to his unattended death by trauma) before I can bring him into my care. We exchange hugs and a handful of words. We do some preliminary planning, and Carey and her husband, Gary, Jason's father, tell me they want to see him as soon as possible. It turns out they unexpectedly passed the scene of his crash on their way home the evening of his death, seeing only his wrecked car and his body under a sheet.

I wonder what I will get when he returns in a body bag. Will it be beyond my skill? A restless night is certainly ahead as I consider what the next day will bring.

I get Jason from the ME's office and onto the table. An autopsy is a messy thing. The organs are in a large red bag placed in the body cavity. This is sealed haphazardly by a few sutures down the large Y-incision made from each shoulder to sternum, from sternum to pubic bone. But this is the easy part. His head is enclosed in another bag, and I won't know what the state of it is until I open it. If what I can offer back to his family is a gift, I'm the first to unwrap it, and it isn't pretty.

In addition to the laceration at the back of his skull (made so the medical examiner could open the cranium and examine the brain) there is a vertical one that runs from the bridge of his nose, through his eye, and stops at the nape of his neck.

The bone in the area is mostly intact. As long as the embalming fluid can reach the tissue, it will firm up enough to hold its shape. But this long gash will take some doing to conceal it. Knowing what's on hand, I'm aware that my suturing cord isn't nearly thin enough to make the closure tight while also not being extremely visible. Leaks are no good, but neither are incisions that look like baseball stitching. I go to the pharmacy in town and find a spool of nylon dental floss.

Unlike a typical embalming with an intact circulatory system, for an autopsied body, each limb is embalmed separately. Not being connected by a heart, they are now independent of each other. Meanwhile, the viscera (the collection of organs) is out of his chest and in a bucket, soaking in cavity embalming fluid. I had to pull out each bundle of organs and make punctures with a scalpel. The rather full intestines and colon will cause decomposition and smells to spread. It is one of the worst tasks, cutting these up to promote preservation.

Now to the head. When the cranium is empty, the vessels that supply the brain are exposed. Before injecting up the carotid arteries and into the face, these vessels must be clamped off so the embalming fluid doesn't pour out inside his skull.

Everything goes as planned after injecting up both sides of the head. One of his eyes is collapsed, but that can be built out with cotton. Closing the incisions running both ways around his skull will take the most time out of everything I do, with particular care needed for the vertical one running up his face.

After suturing the Y-incision closed, I start in with the dental floss and a small, curved needle. Two hours go by as I sit on a stool, bent over Jason's head. Back and forth, pulling the suture tight enough to make a seal, but not so tight that it rips the tissue. All in all, it's close to a five-hour process, maybe more, and that doesn't include getting him dressed and casketed or the time it takes (another hour at least) in which I thinly wax over the incision, stippling for a natural texture, and reproduce the freckles on his forehead with an eyebrow pencil and painstaking attention to detail.

The next morning, I call Carey and Gary. Jason is ready.

Their last experience with Jason was one of horror, stumbling upon their son, draped by the coroner, not knowing what kind of tragedy lay underneath. Now they come to the funeral chapel, and they recognize their son: the slight smirk that could pull into a shit-eating grin is there in its essence. The perpetual tan from working in the sun, clashing with the freckles and naturally fair skin—that's present, too. There's no line of demarcation between the two halves of his head, the bisecting incision being hidden by hours' worth of work. His parents don't know exactly where it is, for which I'm grateful. No parent should have to see that.

This is at the core of why I have learned and practiced this peculiar skill set. Jason is returned for a time. Time enough for his mother to embrace him for the last time. Time enough for his father to lose composure without an audience. Time for his children to come see him one last moment. Time for his friends to fill the church and say farewell. There is time, too, for me to receive a hug from his mother; time to find a place in her heart and realize that she is now in mine.

We have a good funeral, if such a thing can be said to

exist. It's terrible, but there's also the sense that we've done the impossible: we've changed nightmarish imaginings into a reality that, though no less tragic, is no longer marked by chaos and disorder.

Even if the unanimated human body isn't perfectly natural, even if it doesn't seem "right," what has been done is good.

We haven't shied away from the stark reality that a dead body makes clear when its soul is gone. With Jason in front of us, we embrace this frailty. The obvious message that we could all go this same way at a moment's notice is unmistakable. But somehow, in all of it, the process is good. The parents coming to weep with me is good (I can't stay dry-eyed around Carrey). The restoration of a grievous injury is good. The funeral, where the community is able to surround Jason's children and family with support, is good. The body itself is good.

But what if we thought the body was bad, simply something to dispose of and move on from? I'm not sure the impact would be the same. We're more than our souls or our thoughts: our mind isn't the only thing that makes us who we are. Our bodies play an integral role. Jason's massive size, his almost genetic gregariousness that accompanied a large smile—these certainly had an effect on his soul, his thoughts, and his self. His body plays a role in "him," too.

We want our final memories to be "fleshed out." We want them to be as whole as possible, the union of flesh and mind and memory. In the same way that you and I need both our minds and our bodies to experience the world, maybe our loved ones' bodies are needed in order to experience a deceased's memory with more profundity?

It is something to ponder.

A GOOD FUNERAL CAN HAPPEN any number of ways. And while I look to give the gift of a good funeral to all those who are received through our doors, a good body helps.

3

AUTUMN IN NAMIBIA

AUTUMN HAS COME. WE GET a very short season here in the Red River Valley, just a few weeks between summer and the depths of winter, the latter seeming to last the longest. Colorful leaves, ripped from the trees by the wind with a sort of callous indifference, don't get to stay long, not even underfoot, as the snow comes soon after.

While autumn as a season is brief, the shortening days seem somehow even briefer, as the waning daylight corresponds with an increased number of death calls. With a service area of thirty miles in any direction, Mike and I have worked in a lot of cemeteries these few weeks. It is the time of year when I think the cemeteries are at their prettiest. An additional plus is that we are, for this short stretch, neither roasting in our suit coats nor ankle-deep in snow while wearing dress shoes. It is quite possibly the perfect season for funeral services.

More than the weather and foliage, there is something in

the autumn air that makes funerals seem all the more poignant. Maybe it is the fact that Nature herself is in the process of her annual descent into a kind of death, the trees becoming barer as we approach the long regularity of naked branches and white ground.

Autumn is a time best suited for poetry as well as for death, it seems.

Today Mike and I are in Greenwood Cemetery, staking out the dimensions of an upcoming grave. Eight feet long and four feet wide, the actual hole will be a bit narrower, providing a little leeway if the hole dug adjacent to it one day comes in wintertime, when our measurements are less precise.

We're here because the usual sexton (the person who keeps the cemetery maps and records its occupants) is out of town: Mike's long experience in managing the place before Sexton Allyn took the job makes him the one best suited to make sure that Eric's grave ends up in the right spot. It is no small feat. There are plenty of variables with which to contend: the cemetery's multiple maps of mixed veracity; virgin graves that were bought a century ago but never occupied; closed-down roads that were filled in around the 1970s; bodies lying beneath coffin-sized divots, unmarked and forgotten. There is a "roll" to the section where Eric will go that is pleasant to meander through, however inconvenient it is for the ones who maintain the lawn. As we do for the Catholic cemetery (where we are the full-time sextons), we bring a metal detector, tape measures, and utility flags in bright fluorescent colors. We also bring a rake, with a nod to the season, as we work among the leaves and the dead.

We are preparing for an event that has its origins days ago, on the other side of the world.

———•———

THE NAMIBIAN BREEZE BLOWS THROUGH the tent flap. Insects whir, things stir in the grass, and the glow of the fire is dying as the safari guide takes his leave. Another day outside in paradise.

But inside the tent something profound has happened.

A heart that began beating some six decades before in the flatlands of the Red River Valley has stopped while resting in the body that has brought it far from the familiar wheat fields of home. Eric's animating principle has left his now-lifeless body lying on a cot shrouded by mosquito netting. What began as an adventure after a long harvest ends in a reprieve from all the troubles of life.

I don't know it yet, but my next few weeks are being set in motion by this sudden change in being half a world away.

The safari guide notes that Eric isn't up at the crack of dawn as usual, a habit learned from a childhood spent on the family farm, where work begins before daylight appears on the horizon. He finds Eric cold and still, a far cry from his usual red-haired and red-bearded ruddy vitality that has brought him here to hunt big game.

The next steps are taken before anyone in Warren is aware he's gone. Eric's body is removed by the authorities, transported for an autopsy in the capital city of Windhoek, and the necessary details are given to the local funeral home that specializes in "repatriation," as in deporting the body back to its homeland.

That's when I get the call from Eric's brother, Neil, his lifelong companion on the farm.

"Victor. Neil Johnson here. We're going to need you again."

Again.

In the decade on the job in Warren, I've grown closely acquainted with the Johnsons when it comes to death. Neil and Eric's mother last year, their older brother the year before that.

One has to be grateful for familiarities when in unfamiliar territory. Despite not knowing how to proceed, the Johnsons have an understanding that I'll figure it out. We see each other enough around town to have that small-town trust that's built from proximity. They've trusted me with their mother. This time they will hand off another treasured possession—a husband, father, and brother—and in return they'll get to leave the logistics to someone else. A sort of reverse safari guide, bringing the dead home through unfamiliar terrain.

But proceedings aren't as simple as arriving at the nursing home and following the usual flow of things. Repatriation (including embalming and shipping) might be the Namibian mortuary's specialty, but it certainly isn't mine. Yet there are always similarities. The phone calls I might make to the powers that be will always include the time and place of death; there's biographical information needed for death certificates and the fundamental issue of "where is the body now"; these are unchanged. It is that these calls must now cross the Atlantic and the equator.

So begins two weeks' worth of after-midnight calls to Namibia, taking into account the time difference. Neil tells me a phrase he's heard a hundred times while on safari himself: "You people in the States might have the watches, but we have the time." Whereas deathcare moves swiftly in Minnesota, the predominantly Norwegian stock wanting to move on with life, in Namibia people take their time. And this habitual easy-goingness doesn't account for bureaucratic red tape.

I use WhatsApp to call overseas and speak with the consulate and the mortuary daily, setting my alarm for the early hours, when I can catch them to ask if today is the day Eric will begin his long journey home.

In the meantime, I meet with Eric's wife and sons. Lori has been married to her high school sweetheart for forty years. She hasn't changed much from their wedding picture. Her hair is still short and curled, and she still gives us flashes of a smile when the joy of memory outpaces the sorrow of our meeting like this. And while she has always worried when he's away and anxiously awaited his homecoming, this homecoming is surreal, so very different from the others. So final. Eric's normal return (from his last thirteen safaris) brings with it triumphant stories of the hunt, accompanied by pictures of his trophies lolling across his lap or on the ground, juxtaposed with an exhausted smile. Decked out in a wide hat and sweat-stained khaki hunting clothes, he looks even more the part of a farmer than a hunter of the exotic animals we normally encounter in films narrated by David Attenborough.

He won't be returning with his photos from this hunt. He will be returning in a coffin made of acacia wood, its flat lid adorned with a picture of the Last Supper. Lori cannot believe it.

As we lack even the most basic ETA, the first thing we do is discuss Eric's obituary. Outside of the practicalities of having one, it is a good way for his family to reflect on the whole of his life, not simply the last hard days. Stories are told of his childhood spent free-range on the farm and of the subsequent managing of the large operation. We talk of how Eric and Lori met, what their years together held, and what the years that will follow might look like, Lori being grateful for grandchildren and the next generation to operate the farmstead. Two themes boil down in the telling: he loved his Lord and he loved the land. And the fact that he left the soil he so carefully tended to die on the savanna isn't lost on any of us. To quote a line from his obituary:

> *His body will be laid to rest in an African coffin and lowered into the soil of the Red River Valley; the two great works he leaves behind, farming and hunting, as united in his death as they were in his life.*

We will have to meet again to plan his services, but there is no use in doing too much until his body arrives.

And so he does, a few weeks after he drew his last breath. Windhoek to Amsterdam to Minneapolis.

The question that has been on Lori's mind is the same one that has kept me up at night, all the more helpful for making those overseas phone calls, I suppose. Will we be able to see Eric when he returns?

Instead of his family picking Eric up curbside, bags full of safari trinkets in tow, he arrives in the cargo bay, the shipping crate surrounding his casket stamped HUMAN REMAINS in a handful of languages.

After he's driven up north to us, Mike and I open the crate and are met with an unwelcome surprise. Namibian embalming, it seems, is more concerned with practical preservation and not presentation. The high-school-science-lab smell of straight formaldehyde hits us like a solid thing. Indeed, the prep room fans are run at full bore and the door cracked open to let out some of the noxious fumes. Eric is now a body lying flat and stiff with preservatives seeping through the pallor. And for the excellent preservation of his trunk and extremities, his face has received less care. The two of us, choking on fumes, have seen more than we want to, and know we cannot show it to Lori and her sons.

To say no is sometimes a kindness. To leave a wife with only her memories is not my preferred way of memorializing our dead when casketed. I would much prefer to have his many friends and family gather around the acacia coffin and say goodbye, Lori blessing his cold head with a last kiss, his sons closing the lid with their own hands.

As it is, Mike and I clean Eric thoroughly, counteracting some of the formaldehyde smell with a wash of ammonia, then soap, then clean running water. We then shroud him, binding his body not unlike it might have been done had he been lowered into the African grasslands instead of making a series of transcontinental flights home.

We set the meeting to plan his funeral. This one is marked

not by the grief that Eric is still abroad, but by the grief that he is here and yet won't be seen by anyone except myself and Mike. There is, however, goodness found, even here. Eric was a hard-nosed Baptist and a lover of the King James scriptures and sharing the message he gleaned from them with others. With his minister at the table with us, a service is planned that would satisfy Eric's desire to preach the Gospel, both actively from the book and without the use of words. Eric's own gospel on an upcoming Tuesday will be one of love, of a return to his familiar soil, of a sharing of grief between friends, and having a meal together. The simple things that motivate us all—family, food, love, and a desire to give that which is good to another—they're all here.

And so the day comes. Snow has fallen. It has been long enough.

Pastor Hoiseth performs his duties admirably. Eric's nephew and sister-in-law play hymns and special music that I can still hear even now, the old words enlivened by the sheer rawness of their performance. We manage to laugh some on this day of tears, remembering that Eric loved to give advice. I had the opportunity to hear a catchphrase of his: "Here's a little tip for ya," when laying out a design for a family headstone some years back. The connotation is that the hearer is doing something wrong—and maybe I was—but today the tip we are given isn't in words so much as presence. We're all newly reminded by his body lying in its coffin from afar that life is short, so live it well.

We process out of the church and to the waiting hearse. As his coffin bearers give him over to the interior wheels mounted inside the back of the vehicle, I realize they stopped short: the coffin has another two feet to go before he hits the internal stops that tell us he's securely loaded for the drive to the cemetery. I look up and see Lori and his grown children, a huddle of grief for a father taken too soon, a huddle barely able to stand under the weight of its own hugs and tears.

I decide to do it on the fly. I call the family forward. There are questioning looks, some blank looks, some are still letting tears fall. I tell the family to place a hand on Eric's coffin. "Push him the rest of the way in," I coax in something approaching a whisper.

And they do.

Two feet is all it is. That's a third of the depth they say a grave ought to be dug. A trifle. We shift around dining room chairs with greater effect than this. And yet . . .

There's a sort of groan as they push. The coffin isn't heavy. It isn't exertion. Each in the huddle extends an arm. Lori, in the middle, surrounded by her family, pushes squarely on the end of his coffin with what looks to be all the might she can muster right now.

He rolls twenty-four inches and stops.

The huddle pulls away and rises up. The Johnsons seem taller in a matter of seconds. Each person leaving the scrum of their family straightens their back and returns for more hugs. Breaths are deeply inhaled. Eyes are wiped on coat sleeves. I nod at Lori. She takes a son's arm and follows, somehow breathing more easily now than in the last weeks. She reinflates, her walk having a purpose, as I lead her back into the full and waiting church.

We depart for the cemetery after the meal, arriving at the graveside that Mike and I had marked out. The earth is ready to swallow what is left of Eric, a man who is surrounded by his family, lowered into his beloved dirt, and held in his African casket.

Leaves unearthed in the digging blow over the grave after the digger has filled it in. The snow continues to fall on this side of the world, just shy of thirty days after Eric's death.

Come springtime, black dirt will be spread, grass seed sown, and new sprouts will burst into the light upon what was once a piece of cold and barren ground.

Then another set of seasons will come and go, and another, ad infinitum, until the final hour of the final day.

4

A FARMER'S DEATH

MANY OF THE TOWNS THAT surround Warren are even smaller than it is, with three hundred to eight hundred residents, all of whom gravitate here, as we are the nearest hub for groceries and the like. Between each town is ten miles' distance. I once heard from an old-timer that the towns were set up that way in the middle of the nineteenth century because ten miles was about what a person could comfortably walk in a day.

These ten-mile stretches are made up of flat farmland, punctuated by grain elevators, some in use, some standing as memories of the towns that once bustled around them. While the phrase "amber waves of grain" brings to mind rolling hills and wheat, the wheat here is on land so flat you can almost see the earth curve with it. The wheat pays the bills and the sugar beets keep the lights on.

Not having grown up in agriculture, I'm mostly ignorant

of how harvest works and only recently aware of what "custom combining" is. Most people up here are happy to educate an outsider in these things, especially if they have a curiosity about it.

Finding commonalities is also a good way to make conversation. We know a lot of the same people, the average Marshall County farmer and me. We also usually cross paths at funerals, so we really know the same people. Whereas Merle knows Jim (who is currently in the casket) from coffee every morning at the local café, I pulled on Jim's underwear for the last time. Knowing the same people, though intimately in different ways, is kind of consoling to all parties: to me, the fellow farmers, and hopefully Jim, too.

I suppose the thing is that they trust us. Multiple generations come to our funeral home and have certainty we'll put their loved ones into the ground and arrange all the niceties and necessities along the way. We've been at it a long time here.

Chuck DuBore, tanned from daily golf, his silver hair slicked back the same way it has been for decades, still pops by the funeral home a few times a day and shares what he's come to understand since starting here in 1958. Uncle Rudy worked here before him, making our funeral home a third-generation business in a town of fifth-generation farms. Even the local newspaper, the *Warren Sheaf*, has been in the same family since the 1880s. The longevity is part of the deal. One either grows up entrenched in small-town life and then runs far, far away, or one learns a place in the fabric and stays put. Chuck and his family didn't move here planning to stay forever, but Mike did. As the son of an undertaker, he grew up in the funeral home, dusting caskets and washing cars—which is substantially what he still enjoys doing today.

Mike is a fixture in Warren. He gets teased good-naturedly at funerals for not being any taller than he was in middle school, about looking more and more like his dad underneath the goatee. He's as zany as he was in his college days and something of a character. He slips between goofball and genuine compassion with such ease it might give an outsider whiplash. People here know he's the one you call when death knocks at the door.

And while I once thought it would take me decades to become an insider, I melded into Warren easily with a little help. Part of what keeps me here, apart from the practicalities of having a job that allows me to make a living and support my family, is that Mike and Chuck have deep roots that, in some ways, I can be grafted onto. Every town has these roots, and to dig down and find them is to find community and a sense of place and care and comfort, if those are things you seek.

The town immediately to my north (ten miles, as you might have guessed) had a historic car crash in 1978 that rocked the community of Argyle to its core. Four teenagers, all from the same town, all members of St. Rose of Lima Catholic Church, perished together on a Sunday. If you ask someone in Argyle about "the Crash," they will know what you mean. When Chuck walks into that church, decades later, he says he still sees them—the four caskets lined up along the sanctuary steps for their joint funeral service.

Chuck worked for days, embalming and preparing each body, meeting with the individual families to figure out what they were going to do, what roles each would play in this terrible scene. He tells of getting the whole town to sign each of the four guest books, and of the small army of priests (headed by a brand-new bishop) who presided over the liturgy. And though my octogenarian mentor still calls to mind these things, somewhat unwanted, I know that he handled a watershed moment with grace. It's also the case that he (and only he) can relay these moments to me in such detail that they now somehow belong to me, too. This collective memory has been passed on to me, an outsider. I am grafted onto deep roots.

Earning folks' trust is a pretty big part of my job. When I was just starting out in this business in my early twenties, working in a larger community, it was harder. But here, where I am generations-deep simply by having my boss, his dad, and their stories around, I find that trust from the families that reside here comes easy. And I am so grateful for it. If there are things inside me that engender trust between a family and myself, I think there is something special inside them that builds trust, too. Something about the nature of life here colors my work differently in the eyes of the families I serve.

I think it has to do with the land and with farming.

A farmer and an undertaker are not that dissimilar. We work odd hours. And usually they are hours we don't choose. There are a few nights during fall sugar beet harvest when, if I get a death call and am on a lonely black stretch of country highway, I can see all the farmers out in the fields with their lights on. I won't lie, it is my favorite time of year for that reason. That someone other than me is awake, out and working far into the night or during predawn hours. The downside is that the roads become caked with mud, any precipitation makes it dangerously slick, and the ditches and curbs are cluttered with baseball-sized beets that you have to sometimes swerve the car around to avoid hitting.

During harvest we all run hard. Granted, my never-ending season to run hard is less predictable than a harvest, but there's something, too, about working hours that you don't get to choose. My close friend Tom, who is a fifth-generation farmer south of town, says that you never really know what the day will hold. Different plots of land needing different tending—each crop has its own schedule—and fixing broken-down equipment are things that, while unpredictable, farmers can somewhat control. But that's only about 10 percent of the day by his reckoning. The other 90 percent is dictated by the weather. You plan and toil a lot, just to wait for the unpredictable. For them it might be hail, for me it is death.

When I've been able to talk to these folks about the similarities in our work, I'm usually met with a distinct lack of surprise. What I thought was a profound realization is taken for granted. They know all about the unpredictability of the world. And they don't need anyone to tell them that every growing thing comes to an end. In order to replant next year, this year's harvest has to lie lifeless and dried, counted in bushels. Death has little shock value for the guy who grows the grain.

I've thought up a number of reasons why my profession doesn't strike a farmer the same way it strikes other types of people. For one, on the practical side, farmers are integrated into a very small community. These folks have been going to a constant stream of funerals for their elders, parents, friends, and parents of friends since childhood.

When I was going to college in Minneapolis, I always feared and avoided the often-asked question "What are you studying?" If I replied, "Mortuary science," and wasn't asked to elaborate, it was usually met with disinterest. If someone asked a follow-up question, though, and I had to come out with it—"I plan to work with dead bodies as a mortician"—well, this news doesn't sit well with the collegiate crowd. People in their twenties usually have an aversion to death, either choosing to consciously not think about it or it doesn't cross their minds. A typical person doesn't want to talk about death, let alone talk to the guy who's around it so much he can make a living from it.

When I moved here in 2014, as a bright-eyed twenty-three-year-old newlywed, I thought it'd be much of the same. But Warren has been different. When I worked my first funeral in town, people were excited to see who the new guy was. That I was a bearer of bad news, a besuited grim reaper come to take their dead from them, didn't make a single person pause. It seemed they were happy for a new face. My fellow townspeople are comfortable with death in a way I'm guessing most are simply not.

The life of farming trickles into the population at large here. If you're not actively farming, you're either retired from it, were raised on a farm yourself, or as a child visited your grandpa and grandma on their farm. The activity of making the land bear fruit is the same as knowing that what it produces will die. Grain that is still living and growing is no good to us. The only way we can consume it is to have it wither first. Only then can it be ground into the dust that, through some magic, becomes bread, feeds pigs, or makes beer.

The growing, though, is important. It's no different than us, really. Watching children grow is a joy. Seeing your nieces or nephews slowly grow to resemble their parents is a special treat—though it's much scarier if they are your own children, slowly becoming you. This growing cannot go on forever. There will come a point at which what has grown declines. It's all part of living. We don't get to enjoy the growth without the subsequent death. Maybe it can hang as a specter over us, and any one of us can easily let it do that. Death is a powerful thing.

But what if we looked at life like a farmer does? What is it about deeply understanding growing things that makes death somehow more acceptable?

PAUL IS A FARMER, AND Paul is declining. We've watched it happen and I've heard snatches from my friend Mark, Paul's son-in-law. He is in the hospital one day, the next he is in the hospice room of the nursing home. We have an understanding, Mark and I. When Paul passes, I'll be there. While death might come at any time, I tell him that's all part of it. "Call the office," I say, "and if you get the answering service, they'll let me know."

I get the call. I drive around the corner to the nursing home, located conveniently close to the hospital and funeral home. When I arrive, the first person I see is Mark. His eyes are red. He chokes out, "I don't know how you do this," in a clipped tone. He has no other words. We hug for longer than one normally would, and he leads me down the hall to Paul's room. I hug Paul's daughter. I hug Paul's wife, Janet. Then I ask the usual questions: When did he pass? Are we still thinking we'll have a traditional funeral with a casket? When would you like to meet to start planning things?

With these initial matters settled, I discuss transporting Paul to the funeral home. "I am going to take Dad into my care shortly. Would you like to be here when I transfer him onto my cot?" I pause as the family considers my question. "You can help if you like. It is up to you." Mark declines and goes into the hall, as does Janet. Paul's grandson offers to be with me while I move him. I stand beside the bed and pull the sheet over his grandfather's face.

That Paul's big, calloused, currently yellow hands are lying perfectly still beneath the sheet is a shock. That his bushy eyebrows no longer wag, his eyes no longer twinkle. He's not living, growing, changing anymore. Or at least not in the ways we are used to. Whatever this new reality is, it doesn't seem right. This is why his family has left the room.

I roll him toward me and tuck part of the sheet beneath him. I go to the other side of the bed and do the same, shrouding Paul, making a bundle of him that is a little easier to slide over to the waiting cot that I've wheeled up alongside the bed. I tighten the straps that will secure this precious bundle. The cot's pouch is zipped around him, and I poke my head out to let the family know: "We're coming."

Because it is "we." Paul hasn't become an object. He's got

the same bald head, the same barrel chest as he did in life. He's just "at rest," without that particular spark of Paul-ness inside to animate him. His soul is gone, but we've still got his body to attend to.

Paul and I enter the hall. As I roll him ahead of me, I ask the family to follow in our wake as we make our way through the building, then out of it. My silver minivan is parked at the entrance, and with a light touch, its tailgate goes up, ready for me to push him in with all my might. I try not to look too strained. Even if he is heavy, decorum must be kept.

More hugs. After which I close the hatch of the van and slowly drive the few blocks back to the office.

I always try to start embalming right away. I realize fully they're not "going anywhere," but the truth is, bodies always embalm better if their blood hasn't begun to coagulate and their circulatory system congeal. When I get Paul onto the table, I see that he is even more yellow than I previously thought. The low light of hospice rooms tends to hide things like this, and for good reason, I suppose. So, the next step is what I've been trained to do. Jaundice is a damnable thing.

This condition is recognized by the yellowing of the skin due to disease, in this case bile duct cancer. With certain diseases, especially those around the liver, bodies cannot excrete waste efficiently and we get a buildup of a pigment, bilirubin, that results from the breakdown of red blood cells. Bilirubin is usually handled by our livers, but in Paul's case, it is trapped in his skin, causing it to turn almost highlighter-yellow under the unforgiving fluorescent lighting of the embalming room. The best thing to do is try and flush as much of it out as we can, because in an unhappy coincidence, if bilirubin meets the formaldehyde in the embalming fluids, it will convert to its nastier and harder-to-cover-up cousin, biliverdin.

Biliverdin is green.

As we don't want Paul to turn green, I start the embalming with a circulatory flush. There is a neutral chemical I add to the embalming machine's tank, along with a co-injectant that will help dissolve blood clots and promote distribution to and through the capillaries. With any luck, it'll push the bilirubin out of the system along with the blood that is pooling in his body. Mixing up a solution for this purpose (with no formaldehyde), I add a little red dye. If I can get it to reach the outer layer of his skin and tinge it a little pink, any greening I cause will have to occur beneath it, leaving the surface of his skin a normal, ruddier color.

After a successful flush and dye of his face, that most important and identifiable feature, Paul is ready for the process to continue. I treat his hands similarly to his face, opening and injecting down each of the radial arteries so as to control the color of the hands. Hands that have planted thousands of potatoes. Even now I can see dirt in the creases and under the fingernails as I inspect their progress as they shift from yellow to pink. I'll leave the dirt. It seems appropriate.

Attending to the head and hands separately takes time. Could I bomb through it, embalming him as quickly as possible? Yes. But if I do that, the result will be poor and I will be sorely disappointed with it—and also with myself. What am I paid for but to do my best? If Paul could wait four months for his crops to come up, I can wait as long as it takes to do the job right.

Before I leave, I give his face another once-over with the razor where I missed a spot, thin his eyebrows a little with a pair of scissors, and even shave the tops of his ears. Paul was a hairy fella in life, but we want him looking neat—like he did at his granddaughter's wedding.

I meet with the family the next morning and we go through the planning process, the funeral arrangement. The decisions get made, the barnwood casket selected, the details handled. The following day, we get Paul dressed, casketed, and touched up. He'll look his best when we arrive at the church for visitation Thursday evening. Everything has gone smoothly. There's no drama, no wild requests, nothing that will need anything more than my usual standard of care and attention. In short, a traditional funeral in which we can follow the script of meaningful words, perform the necessary obsequies, and do the needful actions, the first of which begins at the church at night and the last of which brings us to the cemetery in the broad light of day.

That night at the church, the same church in Argyle in which the teens of "the Crash" were eulogized almost forty years before, I hear something special that will stick with me. Paul's son gets laughs when he tells this story in his eulogy.

"Dad and I are standing in the field just after returning home from a drive around our acreage. Mom wants us inside, but Dad, who would rather eat a meal in his lap while driving to check on his work, won't be rushed. The sun is setting and we're just standing there surveying the potatoes, nothing more than unidentifiable green shoots at this point. Dad can identify them, though. He's worked with them his whole life, so he can tell the tiniest potato shoot from any other plant. He takes a deep breath and exhales and then turns to me. I'm expecting wisdom, standing there in the dying light of a long day. He smiles at me and says, 'I just like to watch them grow.'"

There is a murmur of laughter. But the simplicity of it hits me bittersweetly, as something that both sums up the man but also sums up human experience. As I think about it, growth is something tangible, lovable. It is also something fleeting. Maybe it is even more lovable because it is temporary?

And isn't that the reality of our own lives? We love a thing all that much more because it won't last forever. Our time in the present is brief, our time in the past is gone, our time in the future is unknown and interminable.

During the night of Paul's visitation, even listening to the eulogy is a temporary thing, a thing that happened in time and is now past. As we go out to the cemetery the next morning, everyone there realizes, whether we put it into words or not, that our time with this man is drawing to a close. Even his body, the now-dead part of him that allowed him to touch our lives, is going to leave us, too.

The life of the potato is meant to end; the life of a person is meant to end. The living thing is cut short so that something new can grow; someone dies and yet something of them lives on afterward. A potato must die in order to nourish us; a person's time is restricted to the present, when they can make our lives richer.

In all of it we can look around us and see life changing and moving, growing and declining. It's part of the cycle, part of what makes us valuable—our ability to touch the present. Just as each plant inhabits its place in a particular patch of earth, we, too, inhabit our place and time. We don't all have to be farmers to embrace the fact that life is temporary, that we don't know what tomorrow holds, and that our greatest gift to others is to make the most of where we currently are.

I think we can become better at growing, at living, and at dying by appreciating not just the profound but the mundane.

Even something as mundane as the potato.

5

WALLS OF CONVICTION

"YOU SHOULD HAVE BEEN A priest!"

It's something I hear a lot in my line of work—something about being in this middle ground between life and death that calls it to mind. We of the funeral-directing sort are both in the homes of our communities and in their places of worship. Having both a semi-clerical role and being familiar with ceremony and offering suggestions about the orchestration of such, the overlap between undertaker and priest is evident and apparently worth mentioning to me on a fairly regular basis. Comments like this used to sting a little bit, but time has softened the sharpness I once felt.

I had always wanted to be a priest.

I have a paper from first grade on which I wrote with an unsteady hand what my dream job would be. The accompanying picture in crayon is of a man in a long black cassock. As a young Catholic boy, from Sunday obligations to family weddings, I could envision myself at the front of the congregation, leading the masses into actions mysterious and somewhat removed from the rest of the folks in the pews. The man standing up there probably knows something I do not. And wouldn't it be a privilege to know it?

As I left boyhood behind, that desire for the priesthood persisted. Whenever someone would ask me, "What do you want to do when you grow up?" I'd answer with something vague, noncommittal, and sheepish, perhaps already understanding in my heart what my brain didn't yet know: I simply wasn't called to be a priest. I didn't have the vocation, no matter how much I wanted it.

It's been said that you don't choose the vocation, the vocation chooses you. A vocation, to me, is the work of one's life that a person is called to do. Not simply an occupation (though it might be), but what the Greeks might call a "telos," a goal. The call to this grand goal is thought of as something external. An external urging from God that manifests itself in a strong internal desire. Or, if you're of the secular stripe, we could think of it as a destiny that is lined up for you, the result of forces outside of yourself and beyond your control. Things like where you live, your family of origin, your life experiences—all these things that you don't choose might be said to be external drivers of vocation.

Whatever you believe, whether a gift from the Divine or a product of sheer determinism, I think everybody does have a vocation. Some kind of role in which the fullest expression of potential creates a harmony between doing and being, giving a sense of purpose.

I was attempting to pick a vocation, a life's work, and was reckoning mightily with it, hoping it would fit me. Especially in my teenage years, rather than wait for the vocation to pick me, I contorted myself to fit in the box I hoped was the right size and said PRIEST on the outside. I said my prayers. I practiced the kind of asceticisms that come with cutting weight for wrestling and offered them for the Holy Souls in purgatory. I kept myself from the natural daydreams of having a wife and family. Despite dating a lovely young woman, I was prepared to enter the priesthood and seminary. I even went to visit a seminary a few times, having some friends who had made the leap.

I enjoyed the fraternity of the place, but found that for all my longing of brotherhood and communal life, the desire to be in the life of a family was stronger. Yes, priests do enter into many families' lives, but it seemed like I was given the desire for a singular family's life, possibly one of my own creation.

The woman I was dating, Paige, later became my wife. She knew of my internal struggle with vocation, and she might have known more about me at that time than I did. For one, she understood my temperament. I am not selfless by nature. I like to receive compliments. The one I like best is "I don't know how you do this." And I'd be lying to you if I said that part of the how I do this is not composed of why I do this. And why I do what I do now is born, at least partially, of selfishness.

For whatever one might think is selfless in retrieving the dead or reaching into a bucket of disarticulated guts that need to go back into an autopsied body, I enjoy being patted on the back afterward. There is never a compliment I won't take gladly.

I want to serve others in what I do, but if I am being honest, I also want to be acknowledged for it.

And working strictly with the body as I do, I have a tangible accomplishment in preparing them and celebrating them, for which I can receive a commendation.

Over time, I have learned how to take these commendations a little less selfishly.

JUDY HAS DIED OF CANCER. It is one of those long-running cancer races. The kind that families describe in an obituary as a "battle." Cancer took the best years of her life, with her dying before reaching retirement, and it also took her hair, both breasts, and a few organs along the way. The last thing it took before rendering Judy lifeless was her identity.

When Mike and I arrive at the house, Judy looks absolutely nothing like herself.

Death can do this to us, even in less extreme cases. We don't usually lie perfectly still. Nor do we do so with our mouths hanging open. Sometimes they hang so wide open it calls to my mind a snake swallowing a mouse. In Judy's case this is all the truer because her neck is rather swollen, and her bald and emaciated skull looks more reptilian than is comfortable.

Her husband, Bill, had been trying to prop her mouth closed for a few days prior to her death, but to no avail. Even the hospice nurse who made it to Judy's bedside before our arrival wasn't able to close it satisfactorily while she gave Judy a final sponge bath, preparing her for travel. After visiting with the family, Mike and I depart with Judy "taken into our care," in this case meaning riding in the back of our minivan.

On the way up Warren's main street, we stop talking about upcoming funerals or things that need doing later and switch to the matter at hand. Judy will be embalmed, and we've got to do everything in our power to make her look good for her family. This is the perennial concern with everyone we handle, but in Judy's case she's still young, in her sixties, and we know her: she's always been rather vain. As it's Mike's day on call, he gets to embalm her. We usually have a policy that we, tongue in cheek, call "My body, my choice." If it is my day on call, I do the embalming and, if I embalm a particular body, I also do the makeup and oversee the person's presentation from when they're on the table behind closed doors to when their family sees them with the casket lid open.

As we went on the Judy call together, it's something of a toss-up. Mike says he wants to run home and get a bite to eat, and if I want to set her features I can. He winks and tells me he doesn't have his cheaters on; not having glasses gets him out of dirty work sometimes. We'll split the job. Being something of a control freak myself, I like how I do things and am happy to make Judy's face resemble her own . . . as best I can.

A week later, we have her funeral, and in the time between her sojourn in the embalming room and her arrival at the church we've gotten her dressed, artfully arranged her wig—a by-product of her cancer treatments—and I've just now mixed a little of her characteristic lip gloss with the makeup for her lips. Mike has let me do the detail work on her face, the reasoning being, I suppose, that I was the one to order her lips and eyes at the beginning.

Her family approaches the casket, certainly dreading what will be a grim representation of Judy that will probably scar them more than her open-mouthed death did.

We stand in back, awaiting the verdict.

"She looks wonderful. Thank you."

EVERY VOCATION PROPERLY UNDERSTOOD SHOULD make things better for those you serve. Especially in the mortuary world. Whatever services we render are an attempt to make life a little bit better for those left behind in the wake of a death.

Each task, in addition to helping someone else, is an opportunity for you to become better in the process. I consider my profession a way to grow in virtue, which in turn makes me better at my job, no matter how tough or menial the task. It creates a kind of positive feedback loop with everyone benefiting in the end.

"THANK YOU. GLAD TO DO IT," I say.

"She really looks like Mom again!"

"Well, she was there the whole time. Half of it is getting her in her own clothes and putting on her lip gloss."

"Please know, we are grateful."

Judy's daughter's face glows as she gives me her impression of her now-no-longer-long-suffering mother's looks. I don't sweep the compliments under the rug, but I've since discovered a bit of truth I didn't grasp before. Judy does look more like herself with her clothes and makeup on, and that carries the water more than my own skills. This is part of the feedback loop. I take the good feedback and pour it back into something else. I use it as fuel the next time it takes thirty minutes to get a mouth "just right."

BUT THE "JUST RIGHT"S OF vocation or beliefs or even the tasks before us aren't consistent. They grow as we grow, and they change amid a sea of setback, compromise, and sometimes standing firm. The constraints accepted alongside our beliefs are just as real as the physical constraints of circumstances outside our control. And sometimes we compromise with the latter.

There are a few families in the area who practice Messianic Judaism. They keep the prescripts of the Torah while also affirming they have been fulfilled by Jesus of Nazareth. Religion invariably intersects with every funeral service in some way, whether staunch or nonexistent, and in this case, we will follow Jewish burial practices.

No metal is to be used to adorn or secure the casket. No embalming is to take place. And burial should be directly in the earth within the fewest number of days possible. Twenty-four hours would be best; forty-eight would do.

Interestingly, Jack, a convert, will be buried in the family plot in a Baptist church's cemetery, way out in the countryside. There isn't an active Jewish cemetery for forty miles. And Jack doesn't fit in there any more than he fits in with the Baptists.

While I don't prepare many Jews for burial, understanding the kinds of firm beliefs that underpin their lives just as my own do, I try to honor Jack's family by managing his funeral as properly and as according to his tradition as possible.

We arrange what we call in the business a direct burial, that is, the burial of an unembalmed body within three days or fewer. The grave digger is called and told he should get to work later this afternoon. I provide the family with a cloth-covered casket. It's made of cardboard and some wood bits, all upholstered on the outside; it has metal handles, but that's it. It's the best we can offer on short notice, being on the very end of the supply chain up here. I recognize the compromise made with what is typically used, a plain wood box, isn't perfect, but it's what we've got.

The cemetery requires an outer burial container to be placed in the grave, as they want to keep the lawn level and safe from collapse in the future. This is a concrete box with a lid into which a casket is usually lowered, a sort of insurance policy against a headstone tipping and the ground sagging. I won't win the battle against the staunchly Swedish cemetery board, so I opt to have the box inverted, lidless, over the casket once it is down in the grave. Jack can go back into the earth unimpeded by a cement barrier and have his concrete "tent" hold up the sod above him. Another compromise, but so be it.

Jack's family is satisfied we're doing what we can, though some of these decisions were looked at askance by the usual funeral-goers, probably wondering what all the fuss was about. But I know the family has convictions.

After we lower him into the earth, the ram's-horn shofar is blown by his grandson, its loud, echoing sound signifying mourning and reflection.

Jack's convictions echo across the flatlands of the Red River Valley.

We do what we can, in life and in death.

BEING A FELLOW CONVICT (of a sort), I am not so much imprisoned by my beliefs as I am contained by them. One of my favorite writers, G. K. Chesterton, imagines this about the containment of walls:

> *We might fancy some children playing on the flat grassy top of some tall island in the sea. So long as there was a wall round the cliff's edge they could fling themselves into every frantic game and make the place the noisiest of nurseries. But the walls were knocked down, leaving the naked peril of the precipice. They did not fall over; but when their friends returned to them they were all huddled in terror in the centre of the island; and their song had ceased.*

Because here's the thing about the walls of convictions. You can climb up them and walk along the ramparts if you wish, seeing the outside world from the higher vantage. If one is contained by these walls, it only helps the beliefs to grow a little in their captivity, gaining what strength they can while sheltered from the world of ebb and flow that waits outside.

I get along best with people who are likewise walled about by their convictions. We might believe entirely different things or even believe in things that are opposed. For my part, I am on regular speaking terms with a card-carrying communist and a forest animist. I have on my speed dial both a Catholic cleric and an agnostic atheist. Believing something firmly provides that foundation on which each of us can build our own little interior castle. Inasmuch as we erect the walls of conviction for ourselves, I think it also builds us a philosophical home into which we can invite another fellow traveler. Were I not to have convictions, I would be, in a certain view, homeless, never offering a safe lodging within my walls or fully empathizing with the well-worn walls erected by another.

And sorting out those convictions and compromises, for others and for myself, is what I believe I am here to do. After much introspection, I came to realize I didn't have the vocation to the priesthood like I had hoped.

But I knew if I wasn't going to be a priest, giving up the dream of seminary, I could pursue the vocation of marriage. As a vocation originates outside myself, I see it as something I have always been meant to do. I was always destined for marriage—I just didn't know it right away. It has since been made clear that my marriage helps me to grow in virtue immensely—especially in those virtues I lack. Do you know how hard it is to be selfish with five people depending on you? And I never knew how much I would grow in my ability to be patient before having four children and a wife, whose need to be earlier than on time is less compulsive than my own.

The practical follow-up issue when faced with the "Now what do I do?" of discerning out of the priesthood is that I also needed to figure out the secondary vocations that were for me. In short, I needed to find a job to support my wife in her desire to stay home with a growing family—a job in which I could utilize my strengths and weaknesses. I had to wade through all these small but glorious compromises and corrections, changes and convictions to find which were most important.

I wanted a job in which I could work with my hands and be proud of my accomplishments.

I wanted a job in which I could talk to people, it being my only marketable skill.

I wanted a job that scratched the clerical itch, but also provided an income.

I wanted a job that could provide me with access to many families' lives, but also give me one of my own.

I wanted a job that had meaning.

And it found me.

Like any major change in life, the decision to pursue funeral service was born of a thousand variables, some not so easy to untangle. It came from attending ten of my own family's funerals in as many years. It was surely wrought from having a baby sister who died and parents who talked about her regularly. My own interest in ceremony played a part, as did my disinterest in math or sales. With these and innumerable influences and compromises in the mix, I'd guess that the final "push" was in a book handed to me by my godfather. A classmate of his,

Thomas Lynch, a mortician and poet, penned a series of essays in a collection he thought I'd like—something both uplifting and serious, a good fit for a young man trying to discern his place. *The Undertaking* struck a chord with me and was the first time I'd seen into the world between the living and the dead. A world I now inhabit.

At eighteen, I sought out a volunteer job at the local mortuary. It began with dusting caskets and vacuuming carpets, attending funerals and handing out memorial folders. It has since become fully grown, with licensure, experience, and some revelations along the way.

As I stumbled into funeral service as a profession with little real knowledge of what it entailed, I found it checked all the boxes. Which both surprised and startled me. There were not a few times along the way in which I thought, *What the hell am I doing here?*

I understood the ceremony and planning part, the semi-clerical half of the job, if you will. But when the first body I saw embalmed was the autopsied body of an eighteen-year-old girl, I won't lie, I had reservations. It was heartbreaking and awful and I could all too easily envision myself or Paige on that table.

Vocation, it turns out, comes with hardship. That early experience in a clinical mortuary setting left me deeply disturbed. But even leaving the funeral home that evening, unsettled and flooded with many thoughts that have now become commonplace to me, I realized I already had the internal fortitude and gifts (waiting to be honed) to someday do myself what I had just witnessed. I could learn this other half of the profession and meld it with my desire to do good, and be artistic, and accomplish something worthy of commendation.

It was shortly thereafter that I came to the conclusion that I couldn't brute-force my way into the priesthood any more than I could *not* do funeral service. Now I feel I must prepare the dead and accompany the living. It seems all too obvious that this is how I will better the world and myself. I've grown to cherish the art and the science, the macabre and the beautiful, and even a bit of the business. It all works together to harness the selfishness I can't yet fully shake and direct it toward something that is about more than just "me."

These days when someone offhandedly tells me, "You should have been a priest," I know what it means. It doesn't mean I missed my clerical dreams. It means I'm in the middle ground, walking between life and death, handling the bodies of the dead with enough grace to touch the souls of the living.

6

GETTING LOST

I HAVE SOMETHING TO ADMIT. When driving for my job, I sometimes get lost. Not in Warren—the town is fewer than fifteen square blocks. No, I tend to sometimes lose my way driving the more than forty miles out to the many country churches and small cemeteries where our services are required.

Land up here is uniformly flat. The only real way-markers are the trees—which look very much the same from one section of farmland to another. Rows of trees, cottonwoods, dogwoods, and nameless bushes and brambles were planted on the prairies by the 1800s homesteaders hoping to block the ever-present winds. This means that for every home built, even if no longer standing, there is a square of trees around a farmyard and then separate tree rows every few miles or so to mark the edges of the property and break up the snow that would otherwise drift feet-high against the buildings. Being as they all look so alike, it is disorienting when things change. Pulling up to Immanuel

Lutheran Church one day I second-guessed myself and briefly panicked that I had gone to the wrong church (again) because something looked "off." The ubiquitous tree row next to the church had been leveled in anticipation of new, less elderly and wind-beaten saplings.

And it is correct to say "gone to the wrong church again." There are two Immanuel Lutheran Churches—and not too far apart. For that matter, there are a lot of little white country churches. While the familiarity of this pastoral setting surely brings comfort to some, to the one driving the casket out to the far reaches of Marshall County, where street signs are a mile apart or more and the landscape is inscrutable, a white country church kind of bleeds into the rest. My fifth year here, when I ought to have known better, I took off for a funeral ahead of Mike, heading west to the church I had in my mind. I could picture it down to the color of the carpeting, vaulted ceiling, and 1990s-era cornerstone. Six miles out of town Mike calls me and asks where the hell I'm going. He waited awhile after watching me turn left out of the funeral home driveway before dialing to see if I'd figure it out for myself. The church we're to be at is due south. And thus, I ought to have turned right.

I had pictured in my head New Hope Lutheran, which looks conspicuously like Angus Tabor Presbyterian. Not little white churches, mind you, but still too similar for my brain to disentangle. That's when I learned a little hack: don't think of the church building itself, but of something else. With two Immanuel, two Zion, and two Our Savior's churches within our service area, it became imperative to think of the people.

All church kitchens look pretty much the same, but the ladies in them? No two are alike. There might be five different church kitchen Mary Anns, but I'd never mix them up. A pulpit is a pulpit, but the ministers in them? They vary widely and, having talked to each a hundred times, are unforgettable. There is something to be said about caring more about humanity than the brick and mortar in which they practice or reside.

But what of those places where there are no bricks, no mortar, and only the remnants of humanity, bodies or the ashes thereof lying in tidy rows under the sod?

If churches are sometimes hard to distinguish or not second-guess, cemeteries are an order of magnitude worse. In a land devoid of landmarks, and knowing that the people are the ticket to my memory, having only dead ones as reminders isn't nearly as compelling. There is less reassurance of landing in the right cemetery when there's no living soul there to confirm I'm in the right spot.

In the age of cell phones, it is rare to be truly and utterly "lost," but it has happened a few times.

Once, on my way to a graveside in Oslo Cemetery (not named after the nearby town, but forty-five miles in the other direction), I got all turned around. Knowing cell service would be spotty, I printed a map that took me to an Oslo Cemetery in that township . . . just not the right one. There was no open grave to greet me in this one, so I stopped where I was, pulled over, and thought about what to do next. Then the vault truck pulled up behind me.

A vault or, more properly, an outer burial container, goes in a freshly dug grave to prevent the casket from collapsing under weight and time. On this day, though, I was on the brink of collapse myself. I had a graveside to set up and I had to be on time. The vault truck driver was new and said he didn't know where he was going, either.

Being somewhat acclimated to small-town life, I figured I'd flag down the next car that drove by on the quiet county highway and ask where to go. Thankfully a pickup truck came along, driven by a local yokel, who was, undoubtedly, already slowing down to crane his neck at the spectacle of a man in a suit waving in desperation, while some other stranger leaned on a parked hearse. While my geography skills might be sketchy, this guy had no trouble. I told him the name of the gentleman to be buried and he informed me that his family was buried in Oslo Pioneer Cemetery. He listed some directions that I jotted down on a piece of paper, but they amounted to something like "Go two miles and turn at the big rock pile, then turn again when you see the farm with the white fence in a quarter mile after that." No street names are used in giving directions up here.

I was just happy he used miles. Residents of the Midwest usually measure distance in time. In the same way I get my bearing about a place from people, there is a kernel of beauty in discussing travel by way of time instead of a unit of length. It seems to embody the idea of enjoying the journey more than the destination. To measure a distance by time tells a person practically nothing about where they are going, but it tells a lot about whom you may want to have on the journey with you or what you'll do in between. Whether it is ten minutes of quiet reflection, a few songs on the radio, or a prolonged internal panic as you drive to a country cemetery, counting time is a valuable thing.

With my paper directions clutched in my hand I lead our procession of two (hearse and vault truck) to Oslo Pioneer Cemetery. The local grave digger is sitting on the hood of his truck, looking impatient and likely wanting to get home for a nap, and it seems he's the only one awaiting us.

It all turns out for the best. There is no rush.

The family got lost on the way there, too.

7

DEATH AT THE RUMOR MILL

WHILE MY VOCATION AND I found each other at the end of high school, I didn't exactly jump right into the death pool. I had my reservations, all based on an early interaction with an established local mortician.

My mother-in-law's family is from a small town in the western part of North Dakota. A German-Russian hamlet with maybe eight hundred people in it, the town sits far enough off the interstate that you have to have it as your literal destination to know it's there. Nobody goes there to sightsee or stops for gas on their way to somewhere else. As most of the people in town are Paige's relatives (at least it seems that way), we used to go there for family functions and events when we were still dating.

At a wedding reception there, I was introduced to the town's longtime undertaker, Bob Schmidt. As he was told in advance that I was looking into the field, we were able to find a seat and chat.

It's an unwritten rule of the mortuary world that, as soon as you get your license, you are obligated to discourage as many people as you can from going into the profession. I can't tell you how many times I heard "Yep. Don't do it. Hours are bad and pay is subpar. If you want something steady that will pay the bills and not keep you up at night, maybe look into accounting, buddy." And while not adhering to this unwritten rule myself, I think there is some sense in it.

The seasoned mortician's first response being one of dismissal or maybe just a description of the harsh realities is justified at times: it keeps the teller grounded, while providing the inquirer with some hard truths. It's good for all of us, from jaded professional to starry-eyed student, to be at peace with the difficulties.

We obviously need people to sign up for this peculiar skill set to keep the profession going and to help handle our dead with dignity and grace. But when I sat down with Bob, I wasn't quite ready for this kind of frank disclosure. It was the first of many dissuasions from a career in funeral service; but that's not what stayed with me. Rather, it was what he told me about practicing in a small town, something with which I'd never had to concern myself.

"I used to bury my friends' parents and that was hard enough. Now I have to bury my friends, and I'm sick of having to do that. I'm selling my business later this year so I don't have to do it anymore."

As I planned on working in Bismarck (population 137,000) or, ideally, moving somewhere much larger, this was a sad thought, but not a pertinent one. I surely wouldn't lead the proverbial "life of quiet desperation" that Thoreau talks about. And I sure as heck didn't want to be that guy someday down the road, growing increasingly more dejected as I put one more acquaintance or friend in the ground. I didn't want to find myself in this job, grow to love it, and then have to quit because of the emotional strain.

And then I ended up where I am now, in a small Midwestern town.

After college, I moved to Fargo (sizable, by North Dakota's admittedly modest standards), where Paige was finishing up college. As we ended up with a honeymoon baby, who attended his mother's university's commencement as a three-month-old, we had a lot of life changes quickly. Paige had a strong desire to be a stay-at-home mother and I wanted to support her in that. Raising our newborn was more than a full-time job. Having to make ends meet with one income, we faced a choice: move to the least-expensive apartment we could find and continue where I was working or try our luck somewhere else where a dollar stretches further.

And then I got a phone call.

As it happens, the funeral world is a small one built on personal relationships, where fellow undertakers in another town or state oftentimes help each other out in a pinch. Throw into the mix casket salespeople, vault companies, and granite shops and it seems that every professional is within two degrees of the other. This phone call I got, from a funeral director in Warren, didn't come as a surprise really. Job offers are always being thrown around. Good help, like with any other business, is hard to find. As a young and competent mortician, I'd fielded a few of these calls before, with none of them being terribly attractive offers from corporate monoliths. This, however, was far from a corporate job. It would be just me and this guy, Mike DuBore, running a funeral home up in Minnesota, where the Canadian border is four times closer than the state capital.

As I considered the job offer, I remembered Bob Schmidt's concerns and the emotional toll this job might take on me. I would get too attached to people in a small town and then regret my life choices and have to quit and move my family away and become a sad accountant somewhere.

The move to Warren would have to be a temporary one.

That was a decade ago.

Job offers have continued to come and go, and even some semblance of internet "fame" for the popular question-and-answer videos I share on YouTube about the various aspects of my job has waxed and waned. All in all, I stay here for a few good reasons.

The first is my great boss. Mike has been so helpful and is an excellent mentor. Not simply as one who has been a mortician for as long as I've been alive, but as a friend and as someone who has taught me how to navigate small-town politics and the rumor mill that keeps the town running and is a double-edged sword. Usually, it's a way to transmit a little gossip, while keeping us all informed of the good things happening—who's had a baby, who's starting a new business, who's a reliable person to call to wire a light or fix a faucet or embalm a body.

Sometimes we're closely involved with the news. "So-and-so has died" is a hot topic downtown and I can hardly go to the grocery store without someone stopping me and asking for the next funeral's date and time. I think locals watch the obituaries closely, whether in the *Warren Sheaf* or on our website, to find their place in our little microcosm. For instance, they have a (probably unconscious) running tally of who is living in town, who has moved away, and who has moved into the cemetery. Like a cycle of accumulation and disappearance that never ends.

THE PHONE RINGS AT FIVE o'clock on a Sunday morning.

This is probably one of the worst times to die, not that any time is particularly great. I dislike the predawn time slot on a Sunday because it usually means rushing what I can reasonably rush at the funeral home, getting home to help dress the kids for church, rushing to church, and then coming back and working at the office after brunch. The day "of rest" gets eaten up quickly when death comes at this hour.

The call that comes in is expected. But not in the usual way. Rumors had been going around town about this death for weeks. That, indeed, Evelyn Kuznia died on the sixth of last month . . . then again two weeks ago . . . and allegedly just yesterday. For reasons unknown to me, Evelyn has been on the grim reaper's chopping block for a fortnight, and she's seemed to slip away to the land of the living each time the rumor reaches our ears. Until this time.

This call is from the hospital, so I am firmly assured that she's gone. Whatever rumors have been swirling about this woman, she's beyond them now. They'll be put to rest tomorrow, when the funeral home's obituary subscribers get an email notifying them of a new one (because that's a thing).

A high school teacher for most of her career, Evelyn was unknown to me, but in the hospital bed, I see a lady who's had a hard run. She's quite emaciated. Her thin, elderly skin is bruised from IV pokes and small bumps that would leave a younger or healthier person unscathed. Cancer has mostly eaten away part of her cheek, leaving a hole through which her molars are visible. The zygomatic arch beneath her left cheek is misshapen and her eye is droopy. She is battle-weary, but at peace now, despite looking quite the opposite.

I get her ready for the funeral, a traditional one in which I'm told the casket lid will be closed due to the hole in her face. I embalm her without taking this into account, as one should prepare each body with the assumption that someone might change their mind and want to see the deceased. It has happened before and will surely happen again. It is likely enough that a family member will make the request to have a last look and say goodbye, and it will turn into a full-blown open casket. Even if this were to happen in the privacy of the funeral home prior to visitation, it's no good having a body unpresentable if plans change. So, Evelyn is shaved carefully, the peach fuzz that has grown on what's left of her cheek is removed. The little hairs that make the short trail from her nose hair to what has become a downy mustache are plucked one at a time. Even if nobody sees her, I can only follow the great advice of Sweeney Todd and send each one I serve to "his maker impeccably shaved."

The important second step—cavity embalming—can be delayed until tomorrow; let it percolate while the cotton packs of the stronger stuff I've put on the cancerous tissues do their thing. No need to rush what can wait.

Later, I will come back to excise with a scalpel any bit of that gristly cancerous mess that is unaffected and sculpt over the whole with a basketweave stitch and some modeling mortuary wax. In the meantime, I've got children to wrangle, and in any case the cotton packs on her cheeks need time to work.

As I get home and wrestle the children into respectable clothing and get out the door with a fit-to-burst diaper bag, I call Evelyn's minister. She ought to know what's going on, and better to hear it from me than surprise her on a Monday, every clergyperson's day off. It goes to voicemail. I leave a quick message. Good enough for a guy carrying one kid around his neck and another under his arm trying to get to church.

Right before the Eucharistic prayer, the phone buzzes in my pocket. It's Pastor Janet calling back. I don't usually answer work calls during my Sunday obligation, but ten minutes later, when my toddler daughter squawks that she's had quite enough of sitting confined in a narrow church pew, I take my leave and let Fiona run around outside. This is double duty now, taking Janet's call and watching my girl fill her pockets with rocks and leaves from the surrounding landscape.

"Hello, Victor, Janet here."

"Hi, Pastor, what's up?"

"Well, you called and left a message and said Evelyn died. I don't know if you've heard, but it's just a rumor. I visited her yesterday."

"Right, yeah, I'd heard that. But she died early this morning and I thought you'd want to know today; maybe tell your congregation during service."

"But it's a rumor, is what I'm saying, Victor. It's been going around for weeks."

"Pastor, I can assure you she's dead. I had her on my table earlier this morning."

"... Oh."

"Pastor?"

"I suppose I should trust you on this one, huh?"

Aside from the rumor mill mishaps, the funeral goes well. Many of Evelyn's friends and former students arrive to pay their respects. Despite being still somewhat emaciated, she looks more like herself than she has in a long time. Death has not passed her by this time, but it's by way of death that she was restored to those who came to mourn her.

Pastor Janet's insistence about Evelyn's cheating of death gave me a smile. Why was Evelyn the subject of such whispering and wild tales of going beyond the veil, only to reappear week after week? What was our town's macabre intent, seeing the woman pass only to revel in each time she seemingly lived on in defiance? What was it about Evelyn that had so many people wrapped up in the singular drama of her demise? For one, "Mrs. Kuznia" was a teacher in Warren for decades, and the interest in her state reflected the simple fact of small-town life that she'd had a significant influence over most of the people who had lived here all their lives (the majority of them). Their genuine concern for her welfare, for the days in which she lived and in expectation of the day that she would die, manifested itself in a great deal of talk around town; talk of what her career in education meant to the hundreds of students who, in the run-up to her funeral, exchanged words over coffee or long-distance calls to those who'd taken up residence in the big city.

Bob had warned me about the tragedy of burying those we know in a small town; and yet here I was surrounded by people fully engaged in mortality, and apparently none the worse for it.

While not everybody becomes central to such rumors as those that surrounded Evelyn, words are shared around town about death almost constantly. Our company Facebook page has more than a thousand followers who keep up with obituary postings and funeral recordings. Our website, as mentioned, blasts out almost a thousand emails when a new obituary goes live. Apart from the curiosity of what's written about our dead after they are no longer here to read it themselves, people want to know their place in town.

In treating the dead, and in seeing and hearing how the community treats them all in their individual ways, I reflect on my own place here, not as a professional, but as an outsider with no local family history. I'm reminded of the pioneers, those settlers who just showed up at a given place—the ones who set out and made a home with only their nuclear family for support and the nearest neighbor miles away through hostile climates or terrains. There are not that many people to choose as your friends in a place like this. It's somewhat like a family in that you're stuck with the characters, so you've got to make the best of it, allowing them (or not) to help shape the course and content of your life.

Some of my "extended family" in Warren are wealthy, some

live below the poverty level. Some are Catholics, some Lutherans, some nonbelievers. All will rub shoulders when we gather at my "house," which is maybe another reason why it's called a funeral home.

In any case, I've lucked out and have some very good friends here. One is a farmer south of town I've mentioned before, Tom, whom I've known since my arrival. Another, a builder. Another is the local lawyer, whom I invited over for a porch beer on a whim a few years back and keep up with regularly. I'm sure I'll make more friends along the way, but we all know where we stand in the mix. When you have a personal connection to each person who comes through the door, both those sitting around the conference table and those lying on the dressing table, it gets harder to disentangle yourself from them. Where a person fits in the fabric of life, what role each plays in the other's, can be difficult to discern when you're linked to everyone.

I know my place in the microcosm. If someone in the family of my few good friends dies, I'll be there no matter what. I cancel plans and rearrange life to be with those whom I love. But part of that is knowing the same would happen if I weren't a funeral director. I consider them close enough personally to cancel plans anyway—that I would get to help arrange a funeral, prepare a body, and work a service are all bonuses. I won't send flowers to the funeral, but I'll attend it as the guy who got a loved one dressed and showed up two hours early to make sure all was right.

A single life touches many, many lives in such distinct and unmistakable ways. Each of those connections creates a web of affection, woven of concern and care, that holds the memory of any one person. My job, in so many ways, is to allow that web one final moment of beauty before the thing held in its center fades from view, the bonds of connection untethering this side of eternity.

I have only a few very good friends in town. I don't need more than that. At worst, I will bury my buddies and their wives. When their parents go, we'll mourn alongside them and give them support. But that isn't something to run away from, but rather embrace being caught in the web of affection.

All this to say, I didn't take Bob Schmidt's advice and I don't think I ever will.

8

GRIM HOUSEKEEPING

MIKE'S CELL PHONE RINGS LOUDLY. He's had the same rock 'n' roll ringtone throughout the decade I have worked here. Owing to his declining hearing, he's cranked up the volume all the way. He pulls the phone from his pocket and tells me with only a glance and the look on his face: it's the sheriff's office. Whenever there's a death at someone's home and the deputies are there to check things out, they always call Mike on his cell phone rather than call the funeral home or go through our answering service. This is made slightly more complicated in that Mike golfs with the sheriff, so the number does pop up socially time and again. In any case, the mind of the mortician always jumps to the worst conclusion. In this case, the worst conclusion is the correct one.

There has been a death across town of an older woman who lives in a house that looks uninhabited, but isn't.

Mike and I pull up and Sheriff Boman steps off the front porch. He tells us Hazel is upstairs and it is "not good." I have walked into plenty of situations like this, where the home is cluttered and dirty. The wallpaper yellowed from both age and clouds of cigarette smoke that seem to still hang in the air. Mike and I go up the narrow stairs with a body bag and a cot.

Hazel is kneeling at the foot of her bed, perfectly stationary. It would be kind of sweet if she died during her bedtime prayers, but I have the suspicion this is simply where she finally dropped. She has had a massive gastrointestinal bleed, as evidenced from the bloodstained sheets, the trail of blood to the bathroom, the horrifying bathroom itself, and the pool of blood that is now puddled between her knees on the worn hardwood floor, across which she'd traveled one last time before falling at the foot of the bed.

She has been dead a little while, so rigor mortis has set in. She stays in the kneeling position no matter what we do as we try to load her into a body bag and onto the cot. We put our weight on her to straighten her out, using the cot's seat belt–like straps to keep her mostly flat. At seventy-five pounds she doesn't fill out much of a shape beneath the zippered pouch; anybody watching our departure won't have too much to gossip about.

When we get back to the office, Mike calls Hazel's son, a classmate of his. Hazel is to be embalmed and the casket will be closed per her wishes. I'm grateful we received this directive. Being as her head was bent down, a lot of blood has rushed to her face, leaving it quite distorted and bloated. Some of the swelling will go down with embalming, but the postmortem staining, the unchangeable purple that comes from busted capillaries, will stay no matter what I do.

Then her son calls to tell Mike that he's on his way to town and will stop at her house to grab some things. He plans to meet with us this afternoon to make proper funeral arrangements.

Rather than begin embalming her, Hazel will rest on the table while I pack what my last employer called a "yuck bag." We load it with all sorts of PPE: aprons, shoe covers, gloves, etc. Mike packs a box of cleaning supplies and tosses a mop, some sponges, and a few rolls of paper towels into the van.

First things first: we have to clean up that house.

This isn't something that is normally in the job description of a mortician. Aftermath cleanup is usually left to another profession. But the fact remains that someone needs to do something, and who better to reenter that rather disturbing scene than the two guys who have seen plenty others like it.

IN THE FUNERAL INDUSTRY THERE'S a fee mandated by the Federal Trade Commission that every family of every deceased loved one is charged. It's nonnegotiable. If love covers a multitude of sins, the "basic services of funeral director and staff fee" covers a multitude of tasks. As we are required to provide itemization for specific goods and services rendered (transportation from the place of death to the funeral home [within fifty miles], $375, for example), everything that is un-itemized falls under the basic services umbrella. This means that much of our overhead and all the stuff I can't exactly put a price on get covered by the $4,000 each family incurs by walking through the door. For a traditional funeral in this part of the country, this amount is about a third of the bill, let's say. But understand, this catchall cost is the most important part of what I do.

This fee covers my time as well as my care. If there's some oddball request, basic services covers it. If I have to fix some kind of random problem (like finding a church organist or breaking up a squabble between siblings), that falls under basic services. It's also where the bulk of my salary comes from. At $70,000 annually, my salary (supplemented by a few side gigs) accounts for a fair portion of the funeral home's expenses. Mike takes his cut, and the rest goes to cover other overhead things like building upkeep, maintenance, supplies, and the hearse. There's a lot needed to keep a funeral home running.

I should note that the hearse is a major expense of its own. Each one is custom-built. Most are Cadillacs or Lincolns, cut in half, extended, and rebuilt to mortuary specifications. Our last one set us back $120,000.

Manufacturers can't sell all that many hearses a year with only twenty-three thousand funeral homes in the country as customers. It also doesn't help that morticians are notoriously thrifty. At DuBore's, we've got church trucks (the wheelie carts for moving around caskets) that have been in our building since the 1950s and are still operational, to say nothing of the rope-pulley elevator out back that carries bodies from the embalming room on the ground level up four feet to the chapel floor. The mechanism will soon be celebrating its one hundredth birthday. If the big player in church trucks is only going to sell to guys like me a single cart every few decades, supply and demand dictates the price goes up. And though the mortuary supply companies charge us an arm and a leg, we're still thrifty where we can be so that funeral costs stay relatively low.

I should note, a funeral bill doesn't reach $10,000 or $14,000 so that I can live in luxury. I live in a three-bedroom home that's coming up on 130 years old. The plaster is just as cracked now as it was when I moved in. We drive a fifteen-year-old minivan that is upholstered mostly in crumbs. I have multiple suits, but only wear them for work. I drive a Cadillac, but only when a dead loved one is in the back. Even Mike, who owns the funeral home, lives in a modest split-level. It is important for us to realize that many of the families we serve live the same way; modesty is key in a job with guaranteed customers. And the truth is, I'd much rather give away something for free than charge a family more than they can pay.

KNOWING HAZEL'S SON IS ON his way, for the next hour Mike and I race through her disheveled house that right now looks more like a crime scene than anything else. I tackle cleaning the bathroom and the vomit-inducing toilet. Mike strips the bed, flips the mattress, and scrubs what blood hasn't already stained the worn-bare hardwood. Do we do a perfect job? Not even close. But could a son, already familiar with his mother's declining housekeeping skills, walk in and not have to know that she slowly bled out all over the second story of the home as she died? It seems passable enough for us. We depart sweaty, but glad we got it done in time.

I daresay most of us wouldn't accept any sum of money to clean up that gruesome mess. It is just one more instance of doing something we hate, but doing it out of love. And so, we charge zero dollars.

9

NIGHT CALL

IT'S NOT UNCOMMON FOR ME to recall the exact time that first call comes in, pinning the emotional connection of a person to the moment I've learned of their passing.

And of all the times I get calls, I might enjoy the peacefulness of a night call more than any other. Most everyone else in town is asleep. There's no traffic under the glowing streetlights. If heading out into the countryside or to the big hospital in the next large town over, I usually can see the eyes of nocturnal critters reflected in my headlights on the drive. Outside of town there's virtually no light pollution: the stars shine, the sky seems bigger. You're closer to nature when it's just you, the darkness, and a deceased in the back of the vehicle.

There's also a clarity of thought that comes with a night call. Being startled awake by the phone and then having to go into "work mode" generates a second wind. Even if I've only slept for a few hours, the rush of being suddenly called to perform an act of compassion and importance sometimes produces the best work. I find I don't trip over my tongue so much at night: words seem to come out the way they were intended.

These reflections come through my head lately. I didn't always have this optimistic view of answering the phone in the wee hours. In fact, for a period of about a year following 2018, I dreaded it.

I'M SITTING IN MY OFFICE as the leaves begin to fall. Thankfully, it's pretty quiet. Nobody has died in my area and there aren't any funerals pending. This isn't springtime with its rush of hangers-on from winter and families trying to lay their loved ones to rest once the ground has thawed. Fall is great that way. The snows haven't come yet, delaying burials and backing up the workload. It is sweater weather. My twenty-eighth birthday is tomorrow. I'll get a meatloaf dinner and have requested a carrot cake for dessert. Paige's culinary abilities are something to marvel at. What's more, three days ago I found out at her obstetrician's appointment we're having a baby girl to join our two boys.

In addition to the conditions being already near perfect, Mike is out of the office: there's nobody around to ask anything of me. I can draw headstone designs or mindlessly browse the web. The world is my oyster.

Then the phone rings.

But it isn't the work line.

A call to my cell phone. Nothing to worry about.

It's my best friend Alex's wife, Andrea. Alex and I have known each other since the misanthropic days of middle school: he was possibly the only person who understood me then. He's always good for a laugh, usually a story at his own expense, and I appreciate his carelessness for circadian rhythms. Alex will take a call anytime, and he's usually up for it if a long chat is needed to keep me going on the final stretch of a night call. We talk about everything and nothing during these calls. I called him right after that doctor's appointment to tell him the news that we're having a daughter.

I pick up the phone with a blasé "What's up, M'Lady?" There is an uncharacteristic period of silence. They live in the remotest part of Wisconsin and have poor reception. But that isn't the source of the pause.

She blurts out in one short breath, "Alex is dead." No introduction, no warm-up.

Alex. Dead.

I find my voice somewhere to ask her how, expecting one of two answers.

Alex always had an addictive personality. If he liked something, he obsessed over it. And this was hard to get used to when we spent nearly every waking moment together. Gifted with a photographic memory (or close to it), Alex recited facts and told stories, trying to get me as invested in the ins and outs of "beating" claw-machine games as he did with the Blues Brothers, John Lennon, or WWE wrestling. This addictive personality manifested itself in less-endearing ways in more recent years. He went from smoking cigarettes at fifteen to weed, to coke, to methamphetamine and narcotics. We'd even had a falling-out for a few years until he got sober.

The first guess I have about his demise is drugs or drinking. He's fallen off the wagon and into the grave.

My second guess, though, is the right one.

Alex has not succumbed to drugs or alcohol, but has taken his own life by hanging.

All the time I've known Alex, along with this obsessive behavior, he's been either on cloud nine or in the gutter. There is no in-between with him. He has the closest of friends (among which I number) and mortal enemies. Some days are amazing, with nothing but laughter to fill them. Other days are filled trying to talk him out of the depths of self-loathing. Never seeking a diagnosis of any kind, all that can be said is that the man is intense. He has lived life pretty damn hard and, now that he's sober, he's all the more intense for it. It just pours out in different ways. Getting married has helped, but he's still hard on himself. Harder than he need be, for what he's already overcome.

I'm having difficulty finding words. I don't know how to talk to his wife, even though I've talked with a hundred other wives dealing with brand-new widowhood, and family members of all sorts going through even closer scenarios. Gunshots, pills, and a few other, more creative ways that folks have ended their lives on purpose are familiar to me. I always find something to say, and it is always imperfect. Half the trick in consoling someone is to simply give them a hug or a squeeze of the shoulder and say nothing, or maybe "I'm here to help." But with Andrea and Alex? There are no words.

"Thank you for telling me," I finally half whisper, half gasp. My eyes sting and begin to swim. I don't hold it together. I say no more. I put the phone down. I lie on the floor so I won't faint. And I cry.

After lying there sobbing a good long time, I call Paige. I tell her I'll be home late. I choke out that Alex is dead and I'll tell her more when I get home. She doesn't push me to disclose more; she is blessedly patient. I then call my parents, who were like parents to him. I call my brothers, who were like brothers to him. My immediate observation talking with my loved ones (our loved ones) is that Alex has somehow slipped irretrievably into the past. Instead of thinking of how Alex is, all of a sudden, within the span of an hour, we're thinking about how Alex was. Our memories are all past tense now; we cannot look forward to making any more of them. Time has stood still for Alex, and time keeps moving sluggishly for me during one of the longest days of my life.

I do my duty to my family, cry a whole lot more, and echo his wife saying the words "Alex is dead" more times than I am comfortable with. It's my turn to hear the shock on the other end of the line.

I know I must call his parents and speak to them. They already know what I know, but I need to hear their voices, just a small bit of comfort we might steal together on a terrible day.

———•———

AS A FUNERAL DIRECTOR, I'M asked my opinion on funerals regularly. Attending a funeral in my own family, people look to me for what to do next, even if there's someone who has planned the event standing mere feet away. If a classmate or friend loses a parent, they, too, ask for advice. Something about knowing a mortician is like knowing a doctor or having a lawyer in the family: we're a trusted professional who gives free consultation or a second opinion.

But this isn't the same. The only person closer to me whom I might have a hand in burying is my wife or children. In order of affections, Alex's funeral is one of the hardest I'll ever have to participate in.

Alex and I grew up together. We came of age at the same time, worked our way through school and first loves, good times and bad decisions, and came out the other side as married men with a future. I kept my future, but Alex could not. He's taken up residence in the past and all we can do now is bring his body home, back to his parents, back to North Dakota.

On the line with his parents, I cry some more. I have practical notions at hand to discuss, though they are somewhat crowded out of my brain by gut-wrenching grief. The main issue that comes up is seeing Alex: his mom has been told they will not be allowed a viewing by the funeral director in Wisconsin. And so, they ask me, "Victor, can you call and ask them why we can't see him?"

I understand why they have been prevented from seeing their son. This is based on what he looks like. Standard for how he killed himself, probably. The standard isn't pretty. He's been unattended in the home for three days. Upon learning this, a stark realization strikes: when I called him to tell him the news about Paige being pregnant with our daughter, that would now be the final time I would hear his voice. And based on when he last spoke to his wife and parents, I was likely the last person to speak to him before he ended his life. I'll just pile this terrible news onto the growing heap of disturbing thoughts in my head that I'll attend to later. Now is the time to hear about his body and report it back to his parents. If anyone can find a way to make this news palatable to them, well, I'm not sure it's me, but it will have to be.

I get the mortician from Wisconsin on the phone. He tells me what I already know. Decomposition has had its way with Alex. Tissues are breaking down without the heart to circulate his lifeblood. Blood pools (we call it livor mortis), tissues retain fluid, and the surface of the skin begins to bubble. Green hues spread, sometimes even turning a bluish color, and postmortem staining is happening, too (when livor mortis begins to leach into the capillaries and break them down, leaving what look like dark bruises). This is all very clinical. The description of a long hanging that I expect. I do my best not to think about these processes happening to my best friend. Who wants to envision what his face looks like, bloated probably, curtained by his long blond hair?

The vision comes unbidden. He's alone. There's blood on the floor from when the ambulance crew tried, in vain, to revive him. He's probably wearing a flannel shirt, sweatpants, maybe his sunglasses are on, always worn inside, irrespective of night or day. I never did see the autopsy or police reports. I don't really need to set the scene more than my imagination already has. Any factual documents will remain unread.

I take what I know for sure, add in my own speculations,

and call his parents. He can be brought back to North Dakota in a casket, but it will remain closed. Our last vision of him, then, is a purely personal reflection that we can spin to be positive and lively. Although, for me, at the moment, it is anything but.

I then help his parents plan a few things about his funeral from a distance: his folks are nearly three hundred miles west of me and I'm six hundred miles from Alex. I don't do the practical business of deciding the time and place, or choosing the casket. I leave that to the funeral director in North Dakota. I do deliver to them a draft of an obituary for Alex. And don't need to ask his parents any questions. I know every facet of his life. Even frivolous things that nobody should have a strong opinion on, like his favorite color of alarm clock (green), are within my ken. I know the dates of his birth, his sobriety, his wedding. I list his family for the survivors' paragraph at the bottom, even the extended ones. I know him. It is what I can give in a time when words at once become both more meaningful and less meaningful.

Words are the only gift I can give Alex now. He's beyond hearing them (depending upon your view of the afterlife), but through his family they come back to him, I like to think. The obituary isn't my only opportunity with words in the days that follow. I'm asked to give his eulogy.

His family has decided to hold his funeral in his dad's hometown some one hundred miles north; Alex has kept company with too much riffraff at home and his family wants distance from them. It is also where the family roots are, a place where their hearts remain, so where better to place Alex? Days later, we (my brothers, another friend, and I) pull up to a small country church, where we are to say goodbye to the Alex who has loomed so large in our memories these last days. I race inside, pull off my coat, and leave it on the floor for my brothers to pick up. I want to see his mom and dad; I want to see what I can see of him. He lives in his parents in the way he lives less fully in me. His presence, his intensity for life, lives in my memory and the memory of his friends, but his face is discernible in those of his parents, and that means something when I know I'll never see his face again except in photographs. And even a picture of him isn't enough. There is a copy in front of me and I can look at the "memorial folder" created for the event. The obituary is in it, somewhat changed from the first draft, the sharp edges of my own misery-fueled writing softened by his mother's intuition. But his picture. It looks exactly like him. Except it doesn't.

His closed casket is at the front of the church, reminding us that he's here with us. He, more willing, it seems, to be here this day than we are. The minister is a ringer—Alex wasn't religious—but he does an impressive job. I've listened to a lot of bad funeral sermons. In the face of youth and suicide, sermons tend to disintegrate. Words become less, the more of them we use at times like these. But this isn't one of those times. The minister rises nobly to the occasion and sends us on with some hope. We ought not forget Alex and remember that, like Jake and Elwood of Blues Brothers fame, Alex is on "a mission from God."

That I am uncharacteristically dressed in all black, sunglasses, and a fedora is no mere coincidence as I pay tribute to Alex via our favorite film, *The Blues Brothers*.

My turn is next. How do I talk about him to seventy-five

people who have gathered? This is where my profession is helpful. It's not in knowing the logistics of how to bring him home. It isn't even in the ability to pull together an obituary at a moment's notice. My professional experience has allowed me to sit through awful eulogies. If words fail the minister, I can tell you that they fail the average eulogizer in a way that's worse.

I walk up to the podium well prepared. I've got a few pages of notes in my hand, half revised at my brother's house the night before. Here's the crux of what I tell his family: what I tell Alex himself.

Alex has taught me about unconditional love. It's a kind of love you learn when you have a friend who enjoys goading you and who frustrates you; a friend whom you can trust to cheer you up, to share an inside joke, or to even look the fool to make you smile; a friend who has lived in your head most of the time regardless of his mortality and now does it in a way that's more raw for the taking of his own life. I tell the assembled that he is the forerunner, the one who taught me this type of unconditional love that I was then able to transfer to the woman who is now my wife. I think two men, two best friends, can love each other deeply in a way that informs all our other relationships. What is grief, I tell them, but the outpouring of great love.

At the close of my eulogy I start to feel a bit lighter. I've done the work I was asked to do. Carrying his casket out with some of our other friends is work as well, and though I am openly weeping as I do it (as I have wept through the whole funeral, aside from the few minutes I pulled myself together for the eulogy), I know it is necessary and unavoidable. When on the job, this action of casket-bearing is about mechanics: How do we get the dead to the next place of ceremony? In this case, though, the mechanics are incidental. I am carrying my best friend to the grave, and I will do it out of unconditional love.

It's a snowy day. The ground is hard beneath our feet in the few spots that we can see it. Indeed, the grave itself will be dug after we leave the cemetery. The earth is sandy and partially frozen, and the grave digger will want to drop the vault into the grave immediately upon opening it. It will be a rush job and kind of messy; no need to have the family watch actions that are mechanical, Alex's remains handled with an indifference unsuitable for their eyes. The casket setup is still on the grave, though. Nobody knows but me that there will be this necessary delay. I am an insider today, whether I want to be or not.

Knowing the grave digger is waiting and that the vault company will have a job ahead of them, after final prayers I grab his wife's hand and we walk away from the grave; we are among the first to begin the slow ride back to the church for a warm meal. Without Alex. We leave him there. And it is strange. He used to come to this town to escape and renew his body and mind when he was feeling low. Now Alex has come to town and his body will remain. He will have several feet of dirt above him, lower than he's ever been before. But I like to think that a part of him sees what we've done and is renewed.

———•———

WHEN I DEAL WITH DEATHS that are a result of suicide, I now know something of the pain that comes with it. We get maybe one self-inflicted death every year. The simple fact that

I buried my best friend has changed my interactions with those who have been left behind after a loved one takes their own life.

Unexpectedly it has also changed my outlook on anxiety and the role it plays in my life.

I returned home from his funeral and found, after going on a night call a week or two later, that I could no longer drive in the dark.

The creeping anxiety of waiting for the phone to ring had always been latent, a sleeping thing waiting to keep me from sleep. But when I got in the car that night, not too many days after Alex's funeral nor too many before Christmas, I was shaking, the walls of the car seeming to close in. I took about a hundred small breaths (not advised) and drove twenty miles per hour below the speed limit, inching my way to the hospital, thirty miles away. When I walked into the deceased's room, I was fine. Just another night call. But when I got back into the car with nothing but an empty road ahead of me and darkness to hem me in on either side . . . it was another agonizingly long, slow, anxious thirty miles home.

I thought maybe it was the snow and icy roads that were causing my anxiety that night. No. In the coming weeks, as the snow lessened and the sky transitioned from perpetually grey to blue, anytime I drove at night I found myself white-knuckling it. And then it started happening when I was driving someplace with my family during daylight. One day I was dealing with life, the next, after laying my friend to rest, I was a twisted ball of stress behind the wheel. I had to do something to stop worrying. I couldn't very well be on call every other night of the year and hope that the phone wouldn't ring. A prayer that people will only die during daylight hours is a foolish one.

Initially, receiving a prescription for Prozac helped in dealing with the symptoms of this new anxiety. Next, I needed to drill down and figure out why this reaction had taken hold and how I could get it to loosen its grip. Yes, it was triggered by Alex, but this wasn't about him, per se. In retrospect I think my feeling of being "in control" was seriously wounded by Alex's death. I was the last person to talk to him and I didn't see his suicide coming. I think I felt responsible at that time for not being aware of what he was going to do. I wasn't in control of it.

My very job was to manage the emotions of death; and suddenly I couldn't.

These thoughts in my head, percolating as I traveled home from death calls and night calls, as rigid in my seat as the deceased was on the cot behind me, I reluctantly admitted I had to talk to someone.

As a person who chats with strangers on a regular basis, it should be easy for me to speak to a therapist, right? They're certainly no stranger to what I'm dealing with, whoever they are. But I put it off, thinking that between recognizing the issue (lack of control) and getting a little serotonin boost (thanks, Prozac!), I'd eventually get through it. I delayed action for three months.

Paige was supportive throughout this time, listening and helping as best she could, but also encouraging me to do the hard thing: to open myself up in such a raw way to a stranger. Me, seek advice about death?

Me, figuratively falling on my sword, realizing that I don't have as great a handle on this as I thought?

I opted for telecounseling. If I didn't have to see the person on the other end of the line, they wouldn't see the extent to which I was suddenly out of my depth when dealing with death.

Thank goodness Robert was kind. We introduced ourselves and I told him what I thought was going on. I didn't want a diagnosis. I knew what was wrong, but didn't have the tools to get myself thinking the right way. I had plenty of opportunities to brute-force my way into driving at night, but I always came out a mess on the other end. What I needed were the techniques to handle this meta-anxiety, to lessen it. I needed to reframe my thoughts—not on driving at night or with a car full of kids, that's the symptom—but reframe my thoughts about death and how it comes when we least expect it.

Over the months that followed in our biweekly discussions, Robert and I talked about breathing, slowing down, positive distractions, and all manner of ways to cope with anxiety. But the thing that I think "cured" it for me was this simple thought:

"Victor, you've driven a car on how many night calls, to how many places; what will be different this time?"

It clicked. I was the professional here. Prior to 2018, I'd been on hundreds of death calls. Each started with a phone call: each ended with me pulling into the garage at the funeral home. There were things in the middle like driving through storms, driving for hours one way, driving at night, but each death call ended with me coming home. If each had the same ending, and I already knew that I couldn't really control it when things did go wrong, why would I worry about that part? The driving was simply a small piece of the large and predictable whole. The beginning, the end, and the uncertainty in the middle. But there was comfort in this idea: it always ended with me coming home.

In short, here is the lesson: I don't have control . . . and I never did. Why it took the death of my dearest friend to learn that simple fact I don't know. But can I be grateful to Alex some years out? I think so. If I want to show him my gratitude I would pass this lesson along, I'd share my story as one who ought to have learned this a long time ago, but didn't.

None of us are in control.

If it is the hallmark of death, it is surely the hallmark of my life.

I can live with it now, the phone always being moments away from ringing.

I can live with driving on a night call, enveloped in the darkness, knowing it is where I must be.

I can live with being in control just enough to do my job when the death call comes in and can live with being out of control just enough to enjoy when it doesn't.

I can live with Alex being dead and I can live with me being alive.

I can live.

I am living.

10

AND A TIME TO LAUGH

WHILE I PERSONALLY HAVE NEVER danced at a funeral, I worked with a family once for whom dance was very important. The patriarch had died and the family wanted dance to be included in the funeral ceremonies. In a high-Lutheran liturgy, there isn't much room for shenanigans, but Reverend Tom was open to the idea enough to include it in the procession into the church. He figured it was before the liturgy proper starts, and there is some precedent in the Bible—and these Lutherans are *sola scriptura* (by scripture alone) through and through.

In keeping with the processional dance craze that was popular at weddings some years back, this family wanted to goofily dance their way to the front of the church, music playing, marking that this was an occasion of joy, a "coming home" and not a "going away." Mike and I would be pulling and pushing the casket ahead of them. A day or two before the funeral we discussed this departure from usual practice, and I asked what dance we should do.

"No dance. Are you kidding, Victor?"

"Do you think we can get away with pelvic thrusts and push the casket with our hips?"

Silence. Then a burst of laughter.

I was kidding.

But the visual was pretty great.

We morticians do enjoy a good joke. Not the one-liner, "I bet people are dying to see you" kind; rather, we like laughing in the face of death. Maybe it is a sort of positive jadedness that comes with the job title, but I have found that, contrary to popular belief, most morticians are pretty funny. They tend to see the bright side of things and even make light of tragedy when speaking among comrades. It isn't gallows humor, either. Really dark jokes aren't all that funny when working on the edge of the narrow chasm of death almost constantly. It is more like we get excited about small things that are otherwise taken too seriously.

My favorite story of this caliber is from Chuck DuBore. I've heard it enough times that I feel like I was there—and I wish I had been. In the 1970s, while he and his assistant were getting a man dressed for his funeral, Chuck was buttoning the deceased's shirt, while his helper got the suit jacket ready. The deceased was a large guy and hard to move, so they needed to cut the coat down the back and sort of drape it over his front. While Chuck finished preparing the dress shirt to rend it, too, down the middle, he heard the clip of scissors and the loud *sshhhrick* of a seam being ripped down the length of a coat.

Then an expletive.

Chuck's helper had grabbed his own suit jacket off the hook by mistake and torn it in half.

While some might bemoan this (as his helper surely did), Chuck still giggles about this storied event so many years out. It is a lesson to remember, but it is also funny, an opportunity to have a good chuckle at some poor guy just trying to dress a dead man. I'm smiling right now thinking about it.

This sort of quiet unconcern for propriety starts early with undertakers. When I was in college, you could always pick out the mortuary science students among the science and medicine buildings. The old and hallowed medical school at the University of Minnesota, Jackson Hall, housed all the anatomy labs and educated numerous doctors, some of whom have since become famous in their fields for advances in surgery and the like. It also houses the mortuary school—in its basement. And while the future oncologists enter with heads held high, starched white coats proclaiming their obvious superiority, the future funeral directors can be found lounging on the steps of Jackson Hall in sweatpants, laughing while enjoying a smoke break between classes.

One might think that mortuary students, of all people, should know better the effects of smoking and drinking. It is true, many of the cadavers in the labs have lungs wracked by the very carcinogens being inhaled just outside beneath the frosted windows. We do, for the most part, know better, but maybe more than most, morticians know that life is fleeting, its pleasures few, and that life is for the living, so have a good laugh while you're at it.

While in school, it seemed the "mortuary blowouts" hosted in my cramped apartment at the end of each semester were some of the best parties I attended in my wilder days. Something about a room of shoulder-to-shoulder men and women who loved life enough to wallow in death made for some lively conversation and enabled a certain laxity of social convention. I won't say much more, but I have a feeling that the "optometrist bashes" were more subdued than the parties of future undertakers.

As I entered my early twenties and started immediately upon the responsibility that comes with a job and family, I quieted down and now rarely drink. I can enjoy two beers at most before the cons outweigh the pros: the morning headache being an unreasonable trade for a lapse in semi-sobriety.

I have taken up smoking again. It's not something I'm proud of. But I figure one hand-rolled cigarette most days (made with beautifully flavored pipe tobacco) is a pleasure that outweighs the small damage to my lungs. In any case, I can still rattle off a few score of push-ups at a crack, am at a low BMI, and can outrun my children without getting too winded. When the scales start to tip, I'll go back to clean living.

In the meantime, it seems my small habit is born from the desire to laugh at death. Not a death wish, mind you, but a simple act testifying that my pleasure in living outweighs the fear of impending doom. This bleeds over to the excitement about small day-to-day things. Things like smiling when putting lipstick on a body that when applied is so bright as to be cartoonish, but requested by the family all the same, or smirking when a minister dusts off the same funeral sermon you heard last week.

It's the small things that one can laugh at when in a dark moment that make us smile in the midst of it all.

Today, the small thing that lightens the mood is neither kitschy makeup nor secret knowledge from having attended too many funerals, but rather movement toward the front of a church, the dancing that seems both out of place and yet very correct.

As Reverend Tom intones from the pulpit, "There is a time to weep and a time to laugh; a time to mourn and a time to dance . . . ," I'm struck with the thought, as I'm nearly tempted to gyrate back up the aisle after depositing the casket and ushering the family into their pews, that maybe those ancient lines aren't opposites, but realities that strike at the same time. It seems right that we can laugh and weep almost in the same instant. The two emotions sit right next to each other at times like these. It is a practice worth encouraging when reflecting on a life or asking a family to share their stories. Both are needed and necessary, laughing and weeping.

And if it is okay to laugh and weep, why not dance and mourn?

11

A BANANA OR A CUP OF COFFEE

I AM THE FIRST TO ADMIT I have not always been affable. That's one of the learning curves of living in a small circle of people: affability is somewhat expected. And it should be.

Nevertheless, we're all human, and I learned early on from Mike that you have to be friendly, all else be damned. Even when you get cornered by the chatterbox at the county courthouse or stuck on the phone with a faceless someone demanding too much of your time, you grit your teeth and bear it. And yes, sometimes the veneer cracks. I've rubbed people the wrong way inadvertently and even a few times been needlessly short on the other end of the phone and hurt some feelings. But apart from these, it was a good lesson to learn: in a small town, friendliness goes a long way.

As I've come to see it, friendliness or affability is a matter of justice, not love. It isn't so much being nice for kindness's sake. It isn't being friendly because life is more pleasant that way. Rather, one ought to be affable because it is what another person is due. Every person commands a certain amount of affability from another for the simple fact that we exist among each other. The same is true for the dead. If we're alive, we deserve affability, and in death we deserve to have our remains handled with respect. And I feel this acutely given that I work in a place where both intersect, where the living involved in a given death are in need of all the more affability, more than the minimum of justice to which we're all entitled, regardless of circumstance.

There's another matter of justice that I have found serves me well in a small town, and it runs alongside affability. That is, I live by the phrase:

"Never deny charity."

It was something I picked up in college when visiting my friends in seminary. They lived in common and had rules about dress and about study, about where they had to be and when. One of the rules that these potential clerics were required to follow while in seminary was to never deny charity.

What does this mean? If someone offers up their charity, a gift or an offer to do something, one should accept it.

You might think that's easy enough. Who doesn't accept something offered to them? Well, a lot of us a lot of the time—and for perfectly sensible reasons. But as I've worked and lived in Warren, I've basically come to say yes to everything.

If someone offers me church-basement food, I always accept—even if it isn't my favorite. If a heavy smoker is pre-planning their funeral and invites me inside the cloud of ash that is their living room for a cup of coffee, I oblige them.

I've had people proffer stale cookies, a seat that was destroyed by a cat, a pocket lint–encrusted baby carrot, gaudy costume jewelry to take home for my wife, and once a banana—as if that were what one customarily offered guests.

Each person who offers me something is asking me to step into their world, however lovely or weird or surprising. Why would I pass that up? I owe it to those around me to understand their circumstances—and maybe the casual banana that's offered will do that.

This decision to never deny charity is good for the giver, I've come to see. I realized early in living with this philosophy that the people offering you things or inviting you to come into their personal world desire good for you. The lint-encrusted baby carrot was from a professor in college who swore they were the antidote for chewing tobacco. That I have never chewed tobacco wasn't the point. He wanted me to know the medicinal effects, and why turn down that knowledge? It's part of giving people what they're owed. If they want to share a baked good that is past its prime over a tannic cup of coffee, it is the giving that's important. Why deny the chance for other people to show charity to me? That they have a different opinion on what I might need or enjoy is immaterial when compared to the spirit in which it is given.

The flip side of never denying charity is that it makes me better at receiving; I am also better equipped to ask for it. If I am conditioned to never say no, why would I worry that other people would deny me help? After all, asking for the charity to move some furniture in my home is related to all the furniture I've carried around for the LOLs (little old ladies) I know. One of my favorite LOLs, Linda, lives down the block from me. When her estranged husband died, she moved back into their marital home—which needed a lot of work. When I'd see her clerking uptown, we'd chitchat, and she mentioned that she had some drywall that needed fixing. I have enough skill to do that passably. Stripping linoleum from the kitchen floor, pulling up carpet, and finding her a respectable plumber followed as a matter of course. If she asked me to do something, I'd try my best to do it. It was an opportunity to do a good turn, the likes of which I would surely ask of another in the future.

ALONG THE WAY, NEVER DENYING charity has led to some interactions I absolutely cherish. As a young funeral director, one of my first solo gigs was the funeral of Helen Hawk. Her husband, the snappily named Harry Hawk, came in with his children to plan the funeral. At the time, this was nerve-racking, to be the person in charge when I was the same age as the next of kin's great-grandchildren. Over the course of the coming days we planned the funeral, attended the Funeral Mass, and laid Helen to rest. It was beautiful to see her family, who had been there as she took her last breath, gather around to wish her a loving farewell.

Harry and I got on well from the start. He treated me like a professional and somehow managed to be grandfatherly without being patronizing. He told me he was proud of me and meant it. In the weeks that followed Helen's funeral, Harry and I kept in close contact. He lived alone now and, with things being so different at home, he would swing by the funeral home on occasion in his station wagon with his dog, Tabby, in the back seat. He asked me if I'd like to have a smoke with him and sit awhile and talk.

Even though this was during work hours, how could I say no to my wizened old buddy who wanted to light up a pipe with rank tobacco and loiter in the funeral home parking lot in the dog hair–covered front seat of his station wagon? That would be denying his charity. We did this a number of times in the coming months and kept up a fairly regular correspondence. I left that funeral home six months later and did my best to touch base before he moved away, too, and we lost contact.

I did, however, slip a note in his file before I left to "call Victor when Harry dies." And the funeral director in charge made good on that. Having two funerals to conduct the day of Harry's, I couldn't make the drive back for it, but I did write his daughter a letter telling her how much her father was appreciated. We would have never developed a mutual fondness, remaining purely professional—I the undertaker, he the bereaved—if I hadn't taken up his humble offer of charity.

As anyone well knows, it is much easier to accept charity from and be charitable to those you like. The grandfatherly gents and LOLs make the giving and receiving of charity easy. The harder thing is to show it to those you don't get along with so much.

There's a guy in one of the towns I serve who is loud, ruddy, and uncouth. I struggle mightily to be nice to him, and sometimes that means avoidance, as it is easier to be charitable from a distance. This means we engage in brief small talk only. If we cross paths, I try to smile and find myself busy with something else in short order. In all reality, he holds nothing against me and is blissfully unaware of my tongue-bitten restraint. His sense of self-worth is untarnished by my secret feelings—and that is good!

"We want to bury everyone—even the idiots" is a phrase I heard uttered regularly at another funeral home in which I worked. And damn if it isn't true. As the only provider of funerals for thirty miles, we want to have funerals to keep the lights on and the door open, but there's also the reality that if not us, then who?

There's something important and humbling about looking out for the people I don't have an affinity for, because as a funeral director, one can't discriminate. Whether I enjoy a person's company or not is immaterial, just as surely as are the questions of what religion they practice, nation they come from, skin tone they possess, or sexual preference they have: none of it has a bearing on what I do. My job is to serve them. And this can be tricky. Much of what I can do for a family comes from what they tell me. Their presuppositions color what they ask of me, like the time I was asked if we serve "people like us," referencing a deceased lesbian partner, or whether or not I, as a Catholic, can serve atheists.

———•———

THERE'S A DISTINCTION TO DRAW here between rendering "service" and making someone "happy." I find that in my earlier years I strove to do the latter, spending a great deal of time conducting a funeral arrangement as if I were taking an order at a restaurant. Most people walk into restaurants knowing what they like to eat, as they eat every single day. Planning a funeral, though, is something you'll only do once, twice, maybe three times in your life. Not only is it a big task, it's one in which your hands-on experience is limited (hopefully). When I was chained to this idea of "making people happy," I would do what was asked, but was often too afraid to do what wasn't asked. I was under this assumption that families knew what they wanted. And if that was true (it's not), I'd just do whatever made them happy without taking the time to get to know them. Because when you do that first, you might realize that what a family needs and what they say they want might be two very different things. When I have been to a thousand funerals and met one-on-one with hundreds of families, I ought to be the one who can sniff out questions you didn't think to ask. I should likewise be able to offer suggestions, anticipate requests, or intuit what is needed better than a family who has planned zero to three funerals. I used to be afraid that if I intuited what a family might need, I could get it wrong. That's a real risk.

Some time ago, I had a family bring in clothing and her favorite makeup for a grandmother who had passed. After getting her dressed and applying her makeup, I couldn't help but notice her fingernails were yellow and chipped and needed a good cleaning. They attracted my attention immediately, that the state of her nails might distract from the positive experience I desired to give her family. Even after scooping out the residue from the undersides, her nails were still a disaster. So, I painted them to match the rather bold color of her lips. Did the family know to ask for this? No. I took the risk. While it may seem insignificant, when they came in and saw the ad hoc manicure, they were pleased. They told me she hadn't worn nail polish since going into the nursing home and that she used to love to get dolled up to do things as simple as going to the grocery store. It was perfect.

That said, I have taken risks and been wrong. Here is a quick example. I design the memorial folders for most funeral services. You know, those little cards or booklets with the obituary and a photo of the deceased, and details of the who/where/when of the day of the funeral. I like to test out new designs when laying them out, often taking inspiration from current trends in the wedding invitation market. If I attempt something new or draw up something I find moving, it is either enthusiastically accepted or flatly rejected; there's no in-between. I once designed a folder after speaking with Rod's live-in girlfriend. She talked about his last days and the hard things at home on hospice, but also the peace that came over them both when he finally departed. For the folder, I made something classic and flowy with script that read *In Perfect Peace* across his smiling picture.

When Rod's adult son arrived, being the one with the right to make decisions as the next of kin, he quickly shot it down and asked that instead it have in block letters: I DID IT MY WAY. These two sentiments couldn't be further apart. I was embarrassed for hitting the entirely wrong note from the perspective of the one who was supposed to be in charge.

Sometimes even with the best of intentions we offer things to people that they simply aren't willing to accept or consider as they might under other circumstances. But to try—both to offer gifts to others and to receive them from them—is a bond we might be wise to strengthen when we can, offering connections to people that often outlive the seemingly trivial acts that forge them. Our time, intuitions, and good intentions can do wonders for others, and make up for some of the many mistakes and personal failings we all have within us.

And whatever our personal failings may be, we want to bury them all with the respect they ultimately deserve. I want to be there to serve and not simply take orders. I want to use my experience to make things better for families. I want to be affable to everyone I encounter, to ask questions and inquire, to be brave enough to ask for help and to offer it, to know my place in the scheme of things given and taken, and to never deny the simple charity of a banana.

12

WHY NOT A BONE ARK?

AFTER FLORIAN DIED, WE BROUGHT him to the cemetery riding in the cab of his favorite tractor. If you have an active imagination like mine, the picture in your head may look funny—an inanimate body piloting a tractor atop its giant wheels. The reality was more sober and moving, if a little disappointing for the more imaginative among us. His grandson parked the tractor outside the church and, upon processing out, he carried his grandfather's urn filled with his ashes to the cab and followed the hearse to the cemetery. Admittedly, it was an unusual funeral procession, and a particularly slow one.

This less-than-usual addition to the funeral plans, however, came at the last minute. The night Florian died, I spoke on the phone to his wife, Josephine, for the first time. Most families I serve at this point know me, if not because I've served them before, then because we've crossed paths in a less formal setting. But getting on the phone with a new widow can be an uncomfortable thing. Her life had changed in an instant. Josephine watched her husband decline for some years and cared for him at home. She'd helped him in and out of his chair multiple times a day, brought him to innumerable doctor's appointments, and stayed overnight in his hospital room with him in his last days: no small feat for an octogenarian. Now she gets a call late in the evening, just after she's arrived home exhausted, from the guy that's going to show up at the hospital and do whatever the next thing is to make a funeral happen.

"Hello, Josephine? Victor from DuBore's here," I say. Her response is cold, and I can't blame her. The next question I ask that will determine my night is whether or not she wants something for Florian that is traditional, with his body present, or whether we want to include cremation somewhere along the way. Josephine is classically Polish. In my area, this means that she "tells it like it is." I've found there is a poetry to the Poles up here (as evidenced by the churches they built and their polysyllabic names) that doesn't translate to late-night phone calls. Direct questions deserve direct answers, I guess.

Josephine tells me, "We don't like fuss. Keep it simple. Cremation right away, I think." I don't press families in this conversation. She says somewhat abruptly that Florian "wouldn't want people looking at him." A common-enough concern.

I'll keep in mind the theme of simplicity as we go through the process, but sometimes when pursuing austerity, families overlook the good or overthink the theme. My goal is to create something both simple and moving—something that won't be "fussy," but also not so bare or sterile that we forget the man who has left us.

It's a strange thing, cremation. For all the talk of the sterility of the funeral home, of the unnatural release of our loved ones to the local mortician instead of taking care of our dead ourselves, cremation brings with it a sterility we don't often consider. The result of cremation is inert carbons. Literal and metaphorical sterility are worth considering. I find that the families I serve rarely know what takes place in cremation, thinking it is some kind of magic that turns Grandma from the jolly ol' troublemaker she was into a jar of dust. And while that is true in the strict sense, for Grandma does become dust, there's more to it, and the gravity of what happens in cremation and the truth of its end result can escape even those of us who are regularly exposed to it: not magic, but a tangible, orchestrated work of reduction.

In cremating a dead human body, a few conditions must be met. Apart from the obvious prerequisite of being inanimate, each body must be in some kind of outer container. A limp and ungainly bundle of a body is hard to manipulate in the retort (crematory oven) and some manipulation is required to make sure everything gets incinerated. I use a type of cardboard casket for this called officially an "alternative container." It resembles an oversized shoebox, but it does the trick.

I write the deceased's name on the lid, the date I will deliver the body to the crematory, and I make sure to note, *No pacemaker, No jewelry*. A body cannot go to the crematory with a pacemaker still in it because the battery can set off an explosion, damaging the retort. And jewelry is best left accounted for and removed.

The boxed-up body heads to the crematory in the funeral

home's minivan. I put down the seats and lay out a wooden dowel. When we slide the cardboard casket in, the dowel rolls along underneath it and will make it easier when we pull it out. The thing about cardboard alternative containers is that they're not terribly durable. I suppose that's the point, but I've had heavy folk in my van without the dowel beneath them and have ripped the tops of the containers out, having to then manhandle the collapsing box out of the van before taping it back up. Even though the body is being cremated, I still shroud it with a sheet in case there ends up being a tear or hole in the box. The raw materials of death aren't always dignified, so I like to at least do that.

Once we have the body out of the van, it'll go on a cart (with rollers and bearings on top) that will weigh the deceased. Like all things, excess weight makes for differing circumstances. A body that has a lot of fatty tissue will, in some ways, cremate itself, the oils in the fat igniting and burning on their own. Knowing the state of a body is very important for a crematory operator to gauge the temperature and time it will take until the body is fully incinerated at several thousand degrees for several hours.

Upon arrival, the body is assigned a tracking number in the form of a steel disk: it is placed in the alternative container (or, rarely, in the full-on casket) with them. The disk that goes in with the body stays with it through the whole process, being double- and triple-checked along the way to ensure that the eventually unidentifiable remains are for the right individual.

Once the body is ready to go into the retort, the crematory operator handles the details. In the end, all the flesh will have been reduced to pure energy and blown out the smokestack, back into the universe—which is not a bad way to think of it, really. The bones that are left are sometimes still somewhat intact—including skull bones, long bones, the femur head being the most visible. The bones, however, have lost their strength. The part of you that kept you upright all your life can no longer withstand a firm squeeze in a clenched fist. One becomes pretty crumbly after cremation.

The next step, then, is to sweep out all these bone pieces into a bin, let them cool, and grind them in a big metal blender into what we recognize as "ash." I use and prefer the term "cremated remains" to describe this pulverized bone dust, which, although a mouthful, is accurate, as they are indeed cremated human parts and are what we have remaining. While not as perfect a euphemism as "pulverized bone dust," at least the term "cremated remains" doesn't refer to the remnants of a campfire.

The remains are then poured into a thick plastic bag, closed with a zip tie onto which the charred metal tracking number disc is strung, and placed inside a hard black plastic box along with the cremation certificate. If burying the remains, some cemeteries will require the cremation certificate along with what we call a "disposition permit." In my state, the health department wants to track a person from the time they die until the time in which "final disposition" occurs. When we bury a casket, this final disposition occurs at the cemetery; with cremation, final disposition occurs at the crematory.

When we get the cremated remains back along with the disposition permit and cremation certificate, we often put them in an urn the family has selected. Sometimes families keep the remains, but up here, we tend to return our bodies, casketed or cremated, back to the earth.

Once in the urn, however, there exists for most people a disconnect. How can a loved one be inside this small vessel? Reality fails. Even I fall into this trap. I can set up a funeral, bring in the flowers, arrange the table with the ubiquitous urn and a picture of the deceased, and forget that this jar is holding someone who used to be of sizable mass. And I'm the one who filled the thing, probably even breathing in trace amounts of the deceased. When we have a casket, this truth about the remains being the person is never overlooked. The reason I think this fact strikes us so obviously is that what remains in the casket is human-sized.

We're hardwired as humans to find the familiar human-sized things either comforting or disquieting—or maybe both at once. If you're somewhere alone, the silhouette of another person on the horizon is either a welcome companion or an impending threat. It is at least recognizable, familiar, and human. And we can see this sort of recognition of human-shaped things everywhere—not just in our dead.

We humans are clunky things. We walk, but we also stumble. We lift heavy things, but also sometimes can't lift ourselves. As someone who moves dead bodies on a regular basis, I can tell you that humans are altogether too long, too heavy, and too floppy to move around with any ease (rigor mortis sets in a few hours after death, lasts for a day or two, then dissolves again, removing any stiffness in the body, and thus the floppiness). There's something to the sheer clumsiness of being human that is both familiar and wholesome. To that point, I think embracing the idea of human-sized things is worth exploring.

When my mom dies, she wants to be cremated. I'll honor her wishes after we have a viewing, as cremation will enable her to be buried in my grandma's grave, her remains alongside her mother's. And that's probably the major benefit to cremation over casket burial in my book. It's not that we'll run out of cemetery space in the United Sates anytime in the next millennium. I can drive to the edge of my town and see acres stretching as far as the horizon that could fit cities of the dead. No, the more important element is the comforting notion that comes with the idea of not just sharing adjacent cemetery lots but sharing the grave itself. Multiple urns fit in a single grave, where multiple caskets generally do not.

But one thing I don't care to do with my mom is bury a jar. I go back to what I was saying, about recognizing the human-sized aspect of humanness, and I think we can do better—or at least offer something different—when it comes to utilizing cremation, while retaining some of the physical presence of the person. I think having a human-sized, clunky thing that kind of arrests us when we see it is vital, cremation or no.

Here is what I envision: a "Bone Ark."

I want the attendees at my mother's eventual funeral service to be caught off guard a little: I want them to remember that they, too, will die and that they might fit in a box as big as a Bone Ark should be. And how big is that? Well, I have this vision of a wooden chest, four feet long, two feet wide, one and a half feet tall. Oaken and roughly human-sized, while also small enough to bury two to a grave. Certainly, it ought to be heavy and bulky enough that one person can't carry it alone—because that aligns with my experience with bodies. While a Bone Ark doesn't have to be as ornate as the Ark of the Covenant, it ought to have rings on the sides into which poles can be inserted to carry it. Cremation often needs ceremony, and so some Ark-bearers (with gloves on?) should march the ark into the funeral service.

I've given much thought to what goes inside the Bone Ark. Rather than bone dust, I think it should be filled with unpulverized remains: that is, after cremation, the identifiable bones should be left intact and placed in the chest. And if we're going to go that far, why not arrange those pieces nicely on a pillow inside the chest? While not everyone might have the stomach to do that last part, I certainly do, and I could do it for Mom—or maybe your loved ones, too, if they were to want it.

Now, before you say I have inhaled too much pulverized bone dust, you should know that there is some precedent for this custom. Cultures all around the world have used ossuaries for their dead. An ossuary is a chest (or even sometimes a whole room) used to store the bones of the dead once their flesh has decayed, rotted, or been eaten or cremated away. One specific example is that of King Louis IX of France (the one whom St. Louis, Missouri, is named after). He died while in modern-day Tunisia on August 25, 1270. Embalming wasn't on the scene yet, and his family, very naturally, wanted his body brought home for burial. Being as it was impossible to bring his rotting body across the continent at the time, they buried his heart separately, boiled off the rest of his flesh, and brought his bones back to Paris in a chest much like what I have in mind. It begs the question: If it is good enough for royalty, why can't it be good enough for my mom?

I can envision my brothers bearing Mom into the church in a Bone Ark, gripping the poles that strain a little under its weight, then setting her Bone Ark on a bier at the front. I can see it getting covered with the funeral pall, candles flickering in the background, and incense wafting up around its edges. I can see us rolling it into the hearse, carrying it out at the cemetery, placing our hands and the hands of our children on it as the final prayers are offered, lowering it into the earth with ropes. The cumbersome humanity of this Bone Ark could bring with it a kind of solemnity and gravitas, not to mention an opportunity for ceremony that is often lost when cremation enters the picture. It would provide some physical work to do, an inconvenience to be sure, but all the same, a last labor of love that we could give our mom who birthed a daughter and three sons into this world.

Despite a Bone Ark only living in my imagination right now, some of these things that swirl in my head I try to work into how I deal with families. Cremation is a tricky thing in that way. In addition to the sterility issue and jar-shaped-versus-human-shaped dichotomy, ceremony is something that gets lost in the shuffle too often. Whereas with a casket, we must have someone carry the thing from place to place and we can't help but realize the human element involved, I find it is often my job to make up for these losses of natural ceremony with some creativity and some sensitivity to ritual.

AFTER ARRIVING AT THE CEMETERY with the giant tractor carrying Florian's remains in tow, his grandson takes the urn out of the tractor and sets it atop the waiting urn vault. The urn vault is a chest of a sort (though not nearly as large or as lovely as I imagine the Bone Ark to be) that I have set up at the graveside, next to the hole that serves as the grave itself. We have closing prayers with the family that the priest leads, and then it is my turn to lead. Without warning the family, I pick up Florian's urn.

While some might consider it rude to handle their loved one without a heads-up, I've honed this practice for some years now. If you tell a family what you're going to do, they often get cold feet or opt not to do the (usually) hard thing. So, I don't give warnings about this anymore.

Holding Florian's urn, I call his immediate family to step forward. They do so hesitantly. I then hand the urn to the child farthest to my left. I say something like "Now as we come to the end, please take a moment to hold Dad and Granddad and say a prayer, give a blessing, or a final goodbye. Then hand it to the next person to do the same." There's no time limit on this. Sometimes you get a hot-potato situation, where the kids can't wait to pass it along. But usually, once someone like me has given them permission, they take their time, despite the eyes of others that are surely upon them. It's an intimate moment that can happen, and here is the time for it. And so, we wait.

I should note that these sorts of intimacies happen spontaneously with a casketed body. People will reach out and touch the wood (or metal), or sometimes throw themselves across it. It seems that we don't need "permission" to interact with something more human-shaped and familiar. I've even had times where, as we leave the funeral and I'm about to close the hearse door, someone yells, "Wait!" and leans in to kiss the casket. I consider it my job to give these same opportunities to the families that don't have a casket before them.

After Florian's urn (or Florian himself, really) has been held, cried over, caressed, kissed, and hugged, all down the line, it comes to the last person. I try to make sure it is the next of kin, so in his case, his wife. I tell Josephine to now place Florian in the urn vault. I assist her by opening the lid, then I extend the offer for those present to "send something with him." (I do let families know about this part in advance so they're prepared.) His family step forward and place in the urn vault Florian's favorite hat, great-grandkids put in crayon drawings of whatever was drifting through their little heads that morning during the service, his rosary goes in, and his wedding ring. Then I pull from my pocket the bolts that will secure the lid. I let his daughters come forward and tighten these with a key. Once our Florian time capsule is closed (though unlike a typical one, these capsules will never be opened once sealed), I ask the sons to step forward. I pull away the board covering the hole in the soil that will soon swallow their dad.

This, too, feels right. Florian farmed his whole life. His entire childhood was spent digging in the dirt, his adult years spent coaxing things to grow in it, and his final times spent watching those same crops flourish—wishing he could be out in the field for one last stretch. And so, he is. Florian is lowered into the earth by his sons, the earth that nurtured every seed placed into it, that caught each footstep, and made up every acre of farmland he tended. The earth is then shoveled onto his remains.

Florian's family walks away feeling grateful (so they tell me later) and fulfilled. There's lingering at the cemetery, but few frowns. The family had done the thing well, accomplished the job, and even gotten a bit dirty, wiping their hands clean on dress pants and skirts. That the grave was opened and now closed is part of the deal. What was left of Florian's body has been laid to rest alongside his forefathers. The children will come back to place flowers; the little ones present that day might remember the sound of dirt thudding onto the urn vault or that they colored a picture for Grandpa to take with him.

We all did something for Florian that day. While not everyone drove the tractor to the cemetery or filled in the grave, each person who had gathered was able to remember Florian and his humanity better because we were given something to do as part of his farewell. The work of handling his remains, of doing or seeing the work done, allowed all of us there to realize that he was indeed present, and it wasn't some jar we were arbitrarily moving from place to place. For a moment, when held in the arms of his wife and children, Florian was visible through the sterility, through the unfamiliar shape, and that is the goal. To take "simple," which Florian's wife, Josephine, requested, and elevate it. To carry out what the family wanted, but also give them what they needed.

I see Josephine from time to time. She's out of the house more now that Florian has passed—though I often see her at funerals. No longer cold to me, now when we see each other I get a hug, or we hold hands while chatting about our families. I was witness to an intimacy with Florian that I helped orchestrate and she hasn't forgotten. What's more, she came in to visit me a year after her husband's death and we sat down and planned her own funeral. In a page and a half of notes I have typed up all manner of requests, from music to what we'll have for lunch, and at the bottom I see my own note.

At the cemetery, do what we did for Florian.

13

DYING AWAY FROM HOME

I AM LUCKY ENOUGH IN my career to have worked with one of Chuck DuBore's oldest and closest friends, Ray Burwell. Ray started assisting Chuck at the funeral home as a part-time helper in 1958. He was the guy Chuck would call at the drop of a hat to lift a heavy body, work a big funeral, or accompany him on a house call. Ray worked full-time for the sugar beet refinery, but somehow managed to slip away and enter the mortuary world when needed.

We joke that there has always been a height requirement at the funeral home. I'm just about five foot nine. Mike is shorter than that, Chuck measures a little beneath him, and Ray held the bottom rung at five foot five. With a full head of silver hair, thick Buddy Holly glasses, and a deep resonant voice, Ray possessed a comforting mien that rubbed off on everyone he encountered.

When we would work together, I'd do most of the actual

work, giving Ray a break whenever possible, as he was in his eighties and slowing down a bit. I'd bring in and set up flowers (which requires more labor than you'd think for something we often consider "frilly" or superfluous) and leave Ray to futz around with the reserved-seat signs, register book, and the like. He'd repay me for taking on the greater labors with a story from his childhood or the navy.

It was a fair trade.

As the years moved on, Ray had to retire from his place as the funeral home's preeminent helper. His memory would get a little fuzzy when we were busy, and we weren't always sure he'd end up driving to the right church in town. And though I lost my chance to spend regular time with him, I did manage to go visit him in the nursing home when he needed more care than living at home could provide. Though his memories of his day-to-day activities oftentimes lacked clarity, he remembered me and knew I had a friendly ear for his stories—even if each punch line or reveal was familiar. One time, I remember going to his rather sparsely decorated room. He said he didn't think he'd be staying long, that he'd die in the bed he was currently lying upon. I got to hold his hand and we got teary together. This is one of the benefits of old age. A person is willing to let their guard down and just be human with you, embarrassment be damned. I asked him if he was scared to die.

Ray assured me that he wasn't scared. He just lamented that he wasn't home.

I'm not convinced that Ray's discomfort in an unknown room is any different from all of ours when looked at from a distance. Everyone, even if on hospice in their own bedroom, in some way dies "away from home." When the human body fails and releases the animating principle that is still very much full of vigor, full of life and stories and things left undone, it seems to me that we each long for some thing, some place maybe, where we can yet complete all that we have left to do and share and be.

Talk to any elder and they will gladly admit that they're eternally twenty-eight in their mind: their deteriorating bodies don't realize that their internal world is ageless. Body and soul are together at that point, but the senior citizen in question wishes the connection weren't so tenuous. Most people have this great internal yearning to remain young and whole, and it follows from my point of view that we yearn not only for this internal world to remain external but also for a place where this can be so. A place beyond our current reality. We long for a homeland we have never seen.

THE GERMANS FROM RUSSIA, WHO populate much of western North Dakota, have a word for this particular kind of homesickness. They call it *Heimweh*.

As a bit of historical backdrop, the Germans from Russia are a group of ethnic Germans who settled in the Black Sea, Volga, and Caucasus regions of historic Russia during the reign and under the protection of Catherine the Great (1762–1796). They kept their language, adopted Russian dress and folkways, and were this odd mash-up of East and West, tilling German-style farms with camels attached to the plows, eating Russian foods, and not paying taxes for a few generations in exchange for making a human barrier against the Tartars. When the great-great-great-grandchildren of these pioneers of the steppes became pioneers of the prairies of the American Midwest, they were culturally out of sorts. They were neither fully German nor fully Russian, nor were they entirely American, either, resisting the proverbial "melting pot" for some time.

Whether on the steppes or a prairie, they would talk of *Heimweh*: a longing for a homeland they had never seen. Early on they longed for the homeland of Germany. Then, generations later, families in America sat in their sod houses and longed for the homeland of Russia. They experienced what I think we all experience in one way or another—we long for a "home" and we feel it exists, but we don't know how to get there. We want something we don't quite know how to grasp. And I have to believe that the long and short of it is that we long for something entirely intangible. Our Home, taken broadly, is something felt by our souls. And our Home is simply not here.

I don't presume to know all the answers about what this Home might look like. I do confidently believe a handful of first things that might help one see death as I do.

I think it is possible for you and me to think wildly different things about what "Home" is with the probability that both of us are wrong. It is likely that our beliefs each point at some eternal, immeasurable ideal, and that one of our beliefs may hit on it more closely than the other—but probably imperfectly at best. Being both aimed at finding Truth, you and I may find we have the same goal, the same endgame in mind: trying to do that which is Good. I also believe that Truth is not alone out there in the cosmos and that this Platonic ideal of Truth is also accompanied by perfect forms of Justice and Beauty and Goodness and Love.

You and I experience these ideals every day. We want Love from our significant others, and we feel slighted when they fall short of it—even if they think they are loving us well. We want to be Just to the people we work with and are indignant when we don't receive Justice in return. Ask a child about Fairness and they will tell you what seems Fair—and as a parent you realize you never sat down and methodically taught them about it: it is kind of innate. If you and I feel a lack of any of these things, or if we know somehow that some things are more True than others, there must be a perfect version of these that we measure against—however inscrutable it might be to us, or however much we might feel we cannot attain it.

And if we recognize these ideals and (maybe wordlessly) strive for them, then there is something inside of us that can touch these ideals despite their intangibility.

And I think that something within us is our souls.

Just as my body can physically grasp a chair and I can feel its solidity with my hands—I can experience the Chair-ity of the chair—it seems only my soul can grasp something like Love. Just like Justice or Truth, Love is something we cannot touch. We say we "feel" Love, but any of us who has fallen head over heels for another knows it isn't a tactile experience. Love isn't simply the racing heart rate and giddy thoughts. It is something more. Even the phrase "making love," while describing a physical action, isn't a perfect example of the experience of Love, for sex is a temporary thing bound in a time and place, and Love seems to have no boundaries at all. You can Love someone who has been long dead. You can even Love someone you've never met.

Being these ideals exist unbound outside of time or place, I firmly believe that when we die, the thing that was able to experience them in this life, this thing we might call a soul, goes to meet them wherever it is they exist. After all, our bodies act the same way. The physicality of our bodies will eventually break down. Our legs will, after years of carrying us about, cease to hold us up, and our bodies will eventually go into a furnace, be put in the ground, or returned to sister earth in some way or another. The chair we sit on (being physical) will likewise lose not two legs but four as it breaks down, its pieces finding their way to the woodstove, the landfill, or the tree row in the back forty to rot into the soil. Our physical reality goes the way of all physical things.

But our soul, which touched the eternal, which experienced Love, which desired Justice, and which sought Truth, will find its way to meet them.

FLESH AND SPIRIT CONTINUE THE fight they've had from the moment they came together. And if disregarding the notion of an ideal "homeland" to which our souls can go, anyone may look inside themselves; the spirit struggles to even be "home" within our own bodies. These cumbersome bundles of muscle, nerve, and bone work against us at every opportunity.

The goal of every person, their body fit or decrepit, might be to grow their soul past the constraints of their body. The word for this is being "magnanimous." *Magnanimity* has its roots in the Latin *magna* (large) and *animus* (soul). To be large-souled is something that is intangible and yet we somehow still see it. I see it.

I have gone to many a bedside and seen the diminished form of a man or woman that emanates a largeness that is at odds with what lies before me under the covers in the nursing home bed. The spirit surpasses the body.

RAY DIED IN 2020.

He has a large soul and one that he always wore on his sleeve. It is on my mind as we get him dressed and Mike and I reminisce about him, pulling his arms through shirt- and then coat sleeves. We might typically use the body lift, a device much like an engine jack, to hoist him into the casket. Instead, Mike and I carry him in our arms to the oak box that awaits him: a box that seems to swallow his somewhat shrunken frame, while simultaneously not being nearly large enough to contain him. His services are held in the cemetery, as gathering in churches is verboten at the time due to the pandemic.

We pray.

I cry unashamedly.

Two uniformed navy men stand at attention in long coats and masks, later folding Ray's flag after taps is played.

It is a privilege to stand at his graveside and help lower his casket into the vault that will hold the body that contained his large soul. It is inverted matryoshka dolls, where the innermost portion is the largest. It is an honor to put his physicality in the place where it will deteriorate, as all physical things do. Ray and I have talked about going home. And maybe the part of him that told me stories and loved me in return is in its homeland, far beyond the reaches of death and decay.

Whatever part I play today, it's a fair trade.

14

WAITING

"**I**'VE BEEN WAITING MY WHOLE life for this."

This line is the single best take on dying I've ever heard. It is wholly true and uncomfortably universal. Each of us knows that this life we lead isn't permanent. We know it is going to end. Each of us will wait a lifetime, and it isn't just the waiting on the front end—for the calls of fate that someone has died—to fill the workload. For the mortician, there is waiting even after death as a body rests and awaits its final rites.

This period between death and services might be as brief as a few days or it may stretch into months—whichever it is, morticians are usually brought into the situation shortly after a death: we work with loved ones to make initial plans for final disposition of a body or arrange a funeral . . . and then sit for four to forty days, waiting for the funeral to roll around so the task at hand might be completed. The reason this period of waiting is toughest is that it can become a period in which the wheels first spin and then fall right off. Too short an interval and it is more about rushing than waiting—and I don't like rushing. Too long a stretch and families tend to spiral, thinking of yet another thing we ought to add to the funeral because "we have the time." There is no good way to bridge this gap in time. It is forever hurry up . . . and wait.

Maybe it's time management and not the waiting that's the trouble? The racing to do things efficiently and legally (like cremating a body within seventy-two hours or so) clashes so wildly with the intervening days that can elapse between when an obituary hits the newspaper and when the stated event is finally carried out. Some tasks must be done immediately, while others drag on. And for all the talk of hopping to my feet at an instant, when waiting upon death as its lowly servant, things can linger on, heedless of best intentions.

A death that we service outside of our thirty-mile radius can be viewed as a case study in waiting. For deaths within a few hours' drive, families generally wait for me to arrive at the place where their loved one died. We have a handful of residents die in Fargo, North Dakota, every year, which may sound positively remote to most of the country, but it is the city in which our largest regional hospital is located, along with the sizable corresponding web of living/dying-related facilities. Though it's two hours one way by car, we do our own work for Fargo deaths: there is a wait.

One of my favorite LOLs died in Fargo during the pandemic. While her body waited for me to arrive, there were a few hours for me to reflect upon my own mortality as the miles passed on the highway. When it comes to my own end, I realize that I am waiting for death with a sort of optimism. But I don't want to "hurry up and wait" when it comes to living, either.

Marilyn Mattson was my neighbor. In her eighties, Marilyn was wildly active and very much concerned with living as rich and full a life as possible. She traveled to all fifty states, toured the world visiting old friends and new places, and was deeply involved with her family. She was a fixture around town, and I think I saw her at most every funeral in my first years in Warren. She always called me "Vic."

Marilyn's red hair was coiffed, never a hair out of place. Her clothes always matched her handbag, and her makeup was always done. Even if just puttering about the yard (which was getting ahead of her in her old age), she'd have on bright red lipstick that was a little wider than the actual outline of her thinning lips. And one tooth seemed to be forever sporting a stray streak of crimson.

I helped bury her husband and am friends with her son, Rick, who runs the local newspaper. I design memorial folders and write obituaries and Rick includes them in the paper. In what is becoming a more and more paperless world, things to hold on to at funerals are important. The *Warren Sheaf* gets delivered to and read by the citizens of my town weekly.

After her surprise trip to Fargo, where Marilyn was being treated in her final days, I speak with her children, most of whom are unable to gather at the time, and plan the funeral. We eventually determine that she will be cremated. Marilyn planned this in advance, but only by a few days. Initially intending to be laid to rest in a casket in the family plot, she could sense that her time was drawing near, that she would not leave the hospital again, and that with the pandemic restrictions in place, waiting would become an inevitable part of the funeral plans. In the days that follow, having ample time to speak with her eight children, a story is told that I cannot forget.

Marilyn's last day is spent writing letters and making phone calls. Each of her children gets a call to tell them she loves them and to offer any parting advice she's gleaned from almost ninety years on this earth. For all the world she has seen, it seems that the small things matter most: her family and the things at hand are what bring her joy on this last day. Having avoided being intubated, Marilyn is on high oxygen as her lungs fail along with the rest of her body.

While I wasn't there for Marilyn's final moments, I am told it went something like this.

She calls the nurse after finishing with the kids. She requests a cup of coffee, brought to her in gloved hands by a masked nurse. She reaches out to grab her Bible, one of the few personal effects she's managed to bring along to what will soon be her deathbed. It lies open on her lap. She finishes the coffee—black, as every good Scandinavian takes it—and looks out the window. She sets the cup down. She smooths her hospital gown—just because she is meeting her Maker doesn't give her an excuse to not look as good as she can muster in that moment.

Marilyn has done her work. She's waited her whole life for this. She's lived to see the world change and change again. She's enjoyed the simple things available to her. A familiar voice, a warm cup, the words of her God before her eyes.

She removes the oxygen tube strung from ears to nose, the one that has been supplying her with life-giving air.

Nature takes its course.

She slips far, far from us, who are now left behind to figure out what to do next.

This is a good death.

A heroic death.

She boldly faced mortality in a time when the world was both afraid to die and unsure of what would happen next. Marilyn left this world leaving each of her children with a gift. Not just of their own lives, but the gift of her graceful death, an example I've yet to see matched. She gave each of them time on her last day and left behind a lifetime of ninety years.

EVEN WHEN I KNOW THE people I care for, as I did Marilyn, the amount of time—however long—waiting with them and their families after death can be a period of hard but beautiful growth.

When it comes to attending funerals, I'm mostly waiting around until the end of the service, when we begin to cover distance. After wheeling or carrying someone into a service of memorialization, I get to sit back as attendees remember their dead. Then, when enough time has elapsed, we're heading back out the door (with the dead in our midst, usually), and it all must go smoothly. That short walk down the aisle for which I wait is critical. The movement is everything.

Because this is where growth happens, in the aisle. This transition from "doing the thing" of the funeral or memorial service to "now our event is done—what next?" is enormous.

At a funeral, when everyone is in their seats and the dead one among us is up front, we're actively completing what we've come to do: honor the dead and remember a life lived. We've planned this event to remember a person and we're all here doing it together, as hard as that can be. The service itself is an important thing, and yet it doesn't encompass all a funeral or memorial can give to one who attends it. Looking backward is vital, no doubt. But then comes the looking forward. The waiting for an uncertain future.

What will life look like now, now that we're slowly making our way to one very literal grave, but also, more figuratively, our own graves? We leave wherever we've gathered the same way we came in—but we aren't the same people as we depart. In leaving a funeral, something changes. We know already that the person we're honoring is gone. We've known it for days as we've waited and have probably talked at length about all the things we'll miss. But then comes the active part of "missing" as we move forward and realize that we're done looking backward. Life is forever altered. The future is open to us, always unknown, sometimes scary, but it is now ahead and there's no avoiding it, whatever it brings. A life has ended, and our own lives continue (or begin anew) in a changed way.

———•———

A FUNERAL EVENT ITSELF IS not the entirety of what we glean from that which follows death, just as a wedding ceremony isn't all there is to a marriage. Yes, we send out RSVPs and mark the calendar with the day and time. Some of us will even inscribe the wedding date on our headstones. Even though my wedding is pivotal, truly the fulcrum on which my own life balances, it was the subsequent walking out into the unknown, hand in hand with my wife on a day the two of us were most alive, that changed me.

This commonality between weddings and funerals exists in many ways, from choosing the date, to alerting and planning for attendance, to arranging a meal to be shared afterward. Is there that much difference between writing an obituary that looks backward and writing wedding vows that reach into the future? Either event pales in comparison to the massive change a family (or couple) is undergoing as departures take place. The unknown awaits us all at these times.

Plato in his *Phaedo* dialogue puts some thoughts on the unknown into the mouth of Socrates. He says that to fear death is foolish. It is foolish because it presumes we know the unknown. We fear death because we fear it is the worst possible outcome. Might not it also be the greatest good? he asks. Death is the great unknown and one can never experience it but to do it: we'll know all about death when we're dead.

Socrates's even-handed optimism is one that I share. No need to fear a thing if it might just as likely be good rather than bad. Hearing about deaths like Marilyn's gives me hope.

From Marilyn, one can learn to properly order one's life. In the same way she attended to her soul, her children, and even her own physical needs (by way of a strong cup of coffee), from her deathbed comes a lesson in self-knowledge.

When I fall victim to my own worries, to complaining about my woes, or embarrassment over the state of the house or how long the grass is around the yard, it is worth keeping the dying's priorities in mind. Yes, a lifetime will contain many concerns and an awful lot of waiting for the unknown to happen. But to know that death will come and to let go of the petty things, embracing it unafraid and unassuming, holding in my mind the things I find dear, is something I aspire to do. Simply waiting for death to happen isn't enough. Growth in life to a state of grace, that is the goal. To move down that aisle toward life and death, embracing the unknown, and having the assurance that, in the end, I might make a good death of my own. That would be a great gift to myself and to those who love me.

So far as I know I'll have some time to prepare. After all, I'll have waited my whole life for it.

15

THE MORT-WIFE

IT IS 6:30 A.M. ON a Saturday. I've been up since two o'clock on a night call, embalmed a body, went home but without enough time to sleep, and am now back at my desk, freshly showered and suited up for the funeral later this morning.

I have done much of the writing of this book at my desk in the funeral home office. To be fair, it isn't "my" desk; rather, Mike and I share it. Because it's a small business, it is usually the case that when one of us has desk work, the other is doing more practical things like moving bodies or meeting with families. That said, time for writing anything but obituaries and death certificate information forms gets squeezed in wherever there are a few minutes to spare. Today it is at 6:30 a.m.

This morning my breakfast will consist of a cup of coffee and a breakfast sandwich from the all-night gas station I passed on the night call located thirty miles east in Thief River

Falls. Warren doesn't have an all-night anything, apart from a funeral home.

My wife is home right now, sleeping. She deserves it after what she's put up with this week.

There's a quote from Groucho Marx that I think of at times like these when I am gone too much and Paige is left without the company of her husband for most of the week:

"Behind every good man is a good woman—and behind her is his wife."

Groucho's quote is more of a quip, but it has some real-life meaning for me.

In my case, Paige is both the good woman and the wife.

Funeral Service is something like the "other woman" in my life.

First, the other woman expects a great deal of time from me, pulling me away from other commitments. My greatest commitment, the one I vowed to Paige, often gets put second to the increasing demands of Funeral Service. And when I'm not actively serving her, she takes up an inordinate amount of space in my brain, keeping me filled to the brim with this week's details and facts concerning the many funerals both in the recent past and those yet to come in the next few days.

It may seem strange to anthropomorphize the profession, but it didn't start with me: Paige dreamed "Funeral Service" into a person early on in our life together. She has told me it is cathartic to direct frustrations about ruined plans and unexpected burdens toward "someone," and it is beneficial to our relationship that this "someone" isn't me. She sees the value, but she doesn't get the accolades. Stay-at-home mothers are already underappreciated in our world. When that stay-at-home mom is a Mort-Wife? Well, it's an added layer of thanklessness.

Let's note that there are a growing number of Mort-Husbands as well, the field's practitioners shifting to more than half women in recent years. In addition to coming in second too often, the Mort-Spouse is characterized by imposed flexibility, the ability to handle a household alone and unexpectedly, and the mental burden of hearing about a job that is equal parts gruesome and emotionally straining, while having little outlet for sharing and coping—apart from repeating it back to the undertaker who shared it in the first place.

The biggest problem my wife finds with the other woman, however, is that she tries to sneakily impose guilt whenever Paige wants to complain about her. For example, this week (as in all weeks), Paige would like to freely gripe about my absence and the inconvenience of meals and bedtimes alone with four kids. But Funeral Service naggingly reminds her that the families that have caused my absence are dealing with the greater inconvenience and permanent absence of death. She admits to wrestling with the complexity of trying to temper her self-proclaimed "dramatic self-pity" without totally invalidating her very real struggles. Additionally, she must be very strategic about the short list of confidants to whom she can vent, never wanting to offend any newly grieving friends or relations of the deceased.

In the last decade, Paige has learned to give herself permission to be frustrated at Funeral Service. It is a terribly nuanced struggle, being upset at your own smaller troubles in the face of death. But it's certainly healthier to let these frustrations out and talk about them rather than bottle them up, because my work's troubles are always around life's most drastic change. I'm grateful we've gotten to this point. For all else that comes with my chosen career, she's been patient and, dare I say it, permissive when the other woman gets in the way.

Paige and I try to have a date night once a month. It doesn't always happen, with my unplanned and random schedule. And when we do go out, sometimes we're third-wheeled by a dead body. For instance, last weekend we went to a party in Fargo. A chance to get out of the house, see some friends, and enjoy a two-hour car ride with no bickering kids or crying toddlers occupying the back seats of the van. But the highway to Fargo passes close to where the crematory is—so a deceased gentleman occupied the back of the van for the first leg of the trip. Yes, he had a slight odor that wafted outside his cardboard crematable container. And yes, Paige put up with the smell and the inconvenience of our crematory pit stop. Just as she's given herself permission to be frustrated with Funeral Service for inconveniences, she's learned to be patient with her, too. Sometimes Funeral Service demands less if we're flexible.

I come home every day I am able to, to have lunch with Paige. The drive home to the opposite end of town where we live takes 3.5 minutes. Some days are packed, but most provide about ninety minutes at home to relax before going back into the fray of the death trade. Days on which there are services held often run over lunchtime. Never knowing when I am going to be home, Paige doesn't heat up leftovers for me, as she is more than familiar with my frequent tardiness. Rather, I'll heat them up myself and we'll have an ad hoc cup of tea if

I walk through the door later than that. This Mort-Wife is not only flexible, she is tolerant.

I once asked Paige if she was bothered with my job—you know, by the things I have to do with my hands? It is a strange place to be, holding hundreds of dead men and women, then coming home and holding my spouse at the end of a long day. Yet as many hands as I hold, both of the dead and often their widows or widowers, my wife's hand is something that the other woman cannot match.

A hundred cold hands are nothing compared to Paige's familiar and reassuring grasp: our palms touching, fingers entwined in the usual way that only couples know; hand in hand, in this together; a Mort-Wife without whom none of this would be possible.

16

KNOWLEDGE AT YOUR FINGERTIPS

EMBALMING IS AN ENDLESSLY FASCINATING subject for me. Some of the nuts-and-bolts details have left me since I graduated from mortuary school, so these days I find most of my "continuing education" in the discipline comes from hands-on experience. Not that this is a bad thing. It plays into the artistic aspect of the process, kind of going by feel as to what chemicals to use and in what quantity for the body that lies on the table.

And for as much as I enjoy the art, I do miss some of the technical knowledge, wishing I could remember it with more clarity. For instance, it is easy to recall the chemical makeup of formaldehyde (CH_2O), but until recently, its microscopic functioning in the embalmed body, apart from the obvious firming I feel in the tissue and the presumed disinfection that takes place, had slipped my mind.

I've got a few more details in my back pocket now, thanks

to ending up in conversation with one of the nation's leading formaldehyde experts. This came by way of my embalming chemical representative, Lincoln, from Dodge Company. I had some technical question about the functioning of my favorite fluid, Chromatech Pink, and Lincoln, being more into the "art" than the nuts-and-bolts chemistry, sent me to Dominick Astorino.

For all my presuppositions about what an embalming chemical expert might be like, Dominick is an easy communicator, breaking down complex chemical processes in a simple-to-understand manner—a nice feature when I've been away from the academic side of things for a while. As we're discussing formaldehyde as a preservative and disinfectant generally, he explains to me how the chemical works after I tell him the following story.

A neighboring corporate funeral home was swamped one day, so I was begged to drive down and do some fill-in work, embalming two bodies back-to-back. This is kind of a fun challenge, walking into an unfamiliar room and being tasked with only the bodies—no families to worry about, no services to arrange. Being able to entirely focus on one task, in cases like these I bring along a bag of some of my favorite embalming instruments, a bit of my own protective equipment, extra gloves so I can wear two pairs at once, a speaker to listen to music (almost always Bob Dylan), and usually a few bottles of various fluids from Dodge I prefer over what the funeral home might use.

The first body was a 103-year-old sister from the nearby convent. She embalmed like a peach, as ladies who have taken perfect care of themselves for a lifetime usually do. Fluid distributed well to fingertips that would be encircled by her rosary when laid out in her habit for her funeral in the cathedral. The second embalming went smoothly as well, this gentleman being a rather portly fellow. If the very healthy embalm well, so, too, do the obese. With large bodies comes large vasculature—and morticians like that a lot when it comes to drainage and tissue preservation. I couldn't have been happier with my work. Until I took my rubber gloves off.

Between embalmings, I always cleanse the table and sanitize the instruments; there are too many blood-borne pathogens that can enter my bloodstream or come in contact with my body. I took off the top messy pair between embalmings, but left the bottom ones on. Sweaty hands are really hard to slide into rubber, so leaving the first set on seemed a good move at the time. I didn't know I had a needlestick through the gloves while embalming the nun. That tiny hole in the left pointer finger of the interior glove let in some embalming chemical—which was then sealed in by the fresh pair.

For an hour and a half, my finger was being embalmed by formaldehyde without my knowing it. When, at the end of the second embalming, all gloves came off, there was my finger, looking Chromatech Pink and hard to the touch. My fingertip "clinked" on the porcelain when tapped on the side of the sink.

I rinsed it for what seemed like forever, crossed two mismatched fingers, and hoped for the best. In about a week's time, my circulatory system had flushed the formaldehyde out and my odd digit softened and returned to normal.

After I relayed this story to Dominick, the formaldehyde

expert told me that though I could see the obvious changes—the firm tissue, pinkish hue, and lack of feeling—here's what happened beneath the surface:

Formaldehyde acts as an enzyme inhibitor. Those enzymes that decompose the body and break down proteins after death do so unimpeded if left to their own devices. If formaldehyde is introduced, it disfigures the protein so that no enzyme can fit it well. When this happens, the formaldehyde breaks down into its respective harmless components (hydrogen, carbon, and oxygen). He told me to think of the enzymes like keys and the proteins like locks; locks being disfigured by the formaldehyde don't "click open" like normal, but stay firmly shut. And that lack of enzyme action and the co-process of killing pathogens are what make a body last, rather than decompose, after an embalming.

My finger, therefore, was preserved and disinfected as well as any dead body until those disfigured proteins could be replaced by my working circulatory and immune systems.

It is always good to have a refresher on embalming chemistry and physiology to support the art side of the process. Though in the future I'd like to keep my hands-on experience away from my fingertips.

17

AN OBITUARY

MIKE AND I ARRIVE AT a home the next town over. We have heard that long-suffering Lynette isn't doing so well, but to our surprise we are not here for Lynette, but for her adult daughter, Jody, who was found dead that morning in the spare bedroom after being up most of the night with her sick mother. She's lying there, looking fast asleep. Except that she's purple. We lift her off the bed and into a body bag and carry her to the cot in the living room, as the corners of the hallways are too tight to get it to the bedroom. We secure her on the cot and carry her out onto the deck, then to the van, leaving dress-shoed footprints in the snow alongside narrow wheel tracks, evidence that someone unexpected has been here this morning.

I meet with Jody's siblings and her son. Lynette has stayed at home, not quite "with it" in the tumult of the day and the days that will follow. Jody's adult son, Nathan, is in charge as next of kin and he seems grateful to have his aunts and uncles there to help. Jody has been living back in Alvarado for a while now, taking care of his grandma. It's a big loss.

In sitting down with Jody's family, I collect the biographical information, but it is scattered. Jody has moved around, leaving her son while she tried to make a new life a few times, none of them really working out like she'd hoped. It would be easy to dwell on these failures, but in the next ninety minutes or so, new stories continue to come up. Odd little things she'd do or say, her propensity to give away the things her family would provide her with to "start fresh." There was a beauty to her lifestyle, a sort of restlessness that kept her on the search for her true home. All we had to do was find a way to word it. Here's what I came up with:

> *Jody lived her life joyfully and had a wanderlust which, wherever it took her, always seemed to lead her back home. After moving to Florida and appreciating every bit of sun she could take in, she moved back to the family homestead with her son, allowing him to have a childhood like hers, with her mother at the helm. She would nurture her own love of independence in him, allowing Nathan to become a very self-sufficient young man.*
>
> *Jody's greatest gift, as well as greatest struggle within herself, was her selflessness, giving all of herself to her family, her friends, several husbands, and anyone else who needed help. Her relationships over the years became life lessons to her son, and she always appreciated being able to give him those tools, despite her own failures in*

marriage. She lived hand-to-mouth but would give away whatever she had. This great spirit of generosity she possessed didn't end with people; she always had an endless parade of animals she was looking after. From dogs and cats and ferrets, to free-ranging finches and fish, Jody always seemed to be able to give a little more of herself to God's small creatures.

The last six years of Jody's life were marked by her usual selflessness as she moved to Alvarado and became a caregiver for her mother.

Jody will be remembered as the life of many a party, a gifted conversationalist, a Sweet Adeline singer, a lefse roller, a dutiful daughter, and a mother that gave her all to her son.

The Lord will provide for her.

It seemed to me the point was to tell her story. To smooth over the negative things and rough edges, but not hide them. Was she absent sometimes? Yes. But she was also by all accounts fully "present" when she was there. Her love for others contributed to her fall, but it is also the thing in her that endures. That's the trick when it comes to writing those last words about someone. Finding the "thing" beneath the stories that made the person tick, the thing that animated them and motivated them, whether for good or bad.

Most of us will be remembered in the hearts of those we knew while they are among the living, and maybe in a few stories handed down by them. It is sobering to think that the average person, living an entire lifetime of hopes and dreams, might one day be forgotten. Each of us has a motivation, a love, and a gritty reality. These are the things that carry on when we're gone, and are hopefully not forgotten.

Enter the obituary: the tangible thing left behind at the end of it all.

I enjoy writing obituaries. I average something like fifty to sixty a year. Multiply that by a lifetime career, and I might have the opportunity to summarize around 160,000 years of human experience. And while the obituary is surely only summary, it is something that lasts long after living memory fades away.

The records in our funeral home office go back to the 1920s, and we've got hard copies of obituaries starting in the 1960s. Prior to that, they're kept in the archives of the local newspapers, but the fact remains that they are kept. Many phone calls come in every year to our small funeral home asking for a copy of an obituary from years past, usually from family genealogists trying to fill in the gaps.

If we are to remember anyone through an obituary long after their death, it is important to write down the things that mattered and that they amount to some kind of truth.

I once had a really lovely funeral arrangement to plan for a woman who was "a character." Somewhat brazen, Elaine told you what she wanted and didn't sugarcoat anything. When I wrote her obituary, I added this fact and the little tidbit that she enjoyed bird-watching, but was absolutely terrified of them up close, alarmed if there wasn't a piece of glass between herself and her favorite hummingbird. When the family received the first draft, they removed the grouchy-grandma part and any mention of her ornithophobia. I thought that was a shame. Elaine had contradictions that didn't need to be hidden. She was a person of dimension. She was funny and interesting in the ways we all are, in ways that make us ourselves.

———•———

IN ADDITION TO BEING HONEST about our grit in obituaries, I think it is important to tell the truth with love. Obituaries need to impart a story in a way that is understandable, sometimes gentle, and not clouded into obscurity by too much euphemism. A balance needs to be struck, though funeral service's greatest reformer, Jessica Mitford, remains in opposition to any and all euphemism. Let me digress for a moment.

Known to all morticians and funeral service workers, Mitford has long been thought of as the harbinger of change in an industry that has been traditionally opposed to it. She wrote a bombshell of a book in 1963 called *The American Way of Death*. When I was in mortuary school, she was discussed with alternating admiration and scorn. Her book was an exposé on the funeral industry at that time, when fees weren't explained, and unscrupulous undertakers were able to take advantage of the unprotected bereaved. This book led to the Funeral Rule of 1984 that mandated funeral bill itemization and transparency. I finally sat down and read this book after years of hearing about it. On some points she was exactly correct: change was needed. On other points Mitford swung her scythe widely, cutting down anything she deemed wrong in the profession.

She writes of euphemism:

> *[The term] Undertaker has been supplanted by "funeral director" or "mortician."... Coffins are "caskets"; hearses are "coaches" or "professional cars"; flowers are "floral tributes"; corpses generally are "loved ones," but mortuary etiquette dictates that a specific corpse be referred to by name only—as "Mr. Jones"; ashes are "cremains."*

Much ink has been spilled about Mitford and the positive changes she brought about, and I'd wager even more has been spilled against her and her polemic.

Whatever the pros and cons, I think her take on euphemism needs more nuance. Language and sentiment unlock the beauty behind the banality.

Words are sometimes used to cover our meaning and obscure the facts. Obituaries are meant to tell the truths of a life and a euphemism can alternately explore beauty where we sometimes have a hard time seeing it. For instance, Mitford's issue with calling a "corpse" a "loved one" darkens the truth. Are not our dead loved? Isn't that the point of a funeral gathering, to pay respect to one whom we loved? I would say that it is almost the defining characteristic of our dead—more than being purely an inanimate body, they are loved; our memories of them linger on and are cherished even though the corpse part of them is now separated from these things. It also seems obvious to me that as professionals we ought to refer to the dead by their names.

I have no objection to being called a "funeral director," as it does, indeed, make up a fair portion of the job. If the title were only "corpse retriever," I'd be depriving my customers of more than half of what can be done for a family when their corpse—I should say loved one—needs handling.

But how do we find the nuance we desire in delicate language when we're very often (and naturally) afraid to venture there?

When we have deaths from drug overdose and suicide, the tendency to want to cover up our vulnerabilities is strong. There's not much beauty to unlock in deaths like these. They seem mostly painful and injurious to those left behind. But the truth can be told in writing them, as a warning to those who might fall prey to the same issues. At times like these, I like to say "ended his life" or "made choices all of us regret." We can tell the truth with love. If we write a woman "died at home," that could mean anything. It could mean she slipped and fell, snorted more than a usual amount of cocaine, or simply didn't wake up that morning. I'd rather we as writers of obituaries not make the readers guess about what transpired, while also not being as blunt as Mitford would ask us to be, which often lacks charity both to the deceased and to the family.

And, to me, charity is the goal. How we ask and probe and offer someone's memory forward in a way that they, though deceased, might accept or recognize it is important.

———•———

AND AMONG ALL THE THINGS we might say or capture about someone, love is hopefully the guiding principle of how we remember our dead. We want to express our love with an obituary. We might say all of what we love about the deceased, their accomplishments, and their grit, while also taking into account their struggles. We should also tell others about the things they loved. These are what make us who we are and help to define us. These things we love echo on after our deaths. And I'm not talking about the love of material things and activities here. There is something of a distinction I want to make between loving a person and having affection for an object or an activity.

I used to make this mistake myself. I would say I "love wrestling," or I "love books." After realizing that love is enduring and that my love of books will only last for as long as I am able to read them with my very mortal eyes, I decided to start using the word "love" more sparingly—using it only for people or for the things that endure beyond this life.

It's a mistake I look back on and I wish I didn't have concrete proof of. An obituary I wrote years ago reads "Duane loved hunting, working on cars, and his family." Two of these things don't belong. Hunting is only seasonal and fleeting; work on a car only lasts for as long as corrosion is kept at bay. I've since been trying to make this distinction clearer. A full exposition of my beliefs during a funeral arrangement isn't necessary, but you can bet that when I write a few paragraphs about Grandma's life I'll write how she "enjoyed" baking, but "loved" the time she spent with the grandkids.

In all reality, the two run together. Grandma liked baking enough to use it to fill her grandkids' bellies.

Whether she realized it or not, it wasn't stirring the dry ingredients together that brought her pleasure. The baking was merely the means by which she achieved the end: showing love to her dear little ones. It was the action that produced the results she desired, the way by which she wanted to place herself within the hearts and memories of those who would love and think about her when she was no longer here. She liked and enjoyed the art of making cookies, but loved the ones to whom they were given.

———•———

WITH SOMETHING AS WEIGHTY AS love and remembrance, like all matters of record today, we must account for authorship. When I write an obituary it's most often crafted from the stories and memories of family and friends of the deceased. I have my interpretations and approaches, but I am merely the hand with the pen.

Could the same be said of a robot?

Not surprisingly, in the age of AI, there is software that can write obituaries for me. All I have to do is plug in the biographical details and the algorithm does the rest. And while I understand that maybe this is a time-saver or that it could be used to create the bones of the thing, which I can flesh out later, I'm still skeptical.

Saving time is a fine thing, but what are families paying me for but my time? Time is the gift. Nobody is interested in how fast a thing gets done in the funeral world: it's the fact of it being done well that fortifies a reputation and brings satisfaction to a family and the undertaker who serves them.

But it's nevertheless an interesting question of how we

all want to be remembered, and what pertinent truths and insights—whoever or whatever organizes them into a coherent narrative—we wish to see bundled with our memory.

I am among those who have a strong desire to consider and share our own obituary, our life summarized—at least as it stands today. This is something I do regularly, updating my obituary each August.

And I find that when I do update it, it gets shorter each year. Not that I've accomplished less; I think I just realize that the most important things aren't those I have done, but rather those things I have loved. My beliefs, marriage, children, work, and interests take precedence—hopefully in that order.

VICTOR MURPHY SWEENEY was born three months premature in November of 1990, in Royal Oak, MI, the second child of Robert V. and Michelle Sweeney. He spent his youth in Michigan, enjoying a great deal of time with his maternal grandmother, MeMe, and his great-grandparents Vic and Ruby. Growing up, he alternately bullied and befriended his two brothers, Vince and Ben. In 2000, the family moved to Dublin, OH; and in 2003, they moved again, to Bismarck, ND.

The move to Bismarck was a culture shock, but eventually Victor considered it "home," where all his formative years were spent. A transfer to St. Mary's Central High School after his freshman year changed his life dramatically. He learned the meaning of true Catholic manhood from his mentor, Mr. Jerome Richter. He also came to know his calling to be a funeral director after discerning out of a desire to become a priest, which he'd had since childhood.

The shining moment of Victor's experience at St. Mary's was in 2007, when Paige Willey said, "Sure," when he asked her to a school dance. Fast-forward through six years, schooling in Cork, Ireland, and at the University of Minnesota in Minneapolis, to July 13, 2013, when they were married by Victor's godfather, Fr. James Hurlbert (who also baptized him as a baby).

In July of 2014, Victor moved with his wife and newborn son to Warren, MN, where he worked at DuBore Funeral Home, serving the many families there and pursuing his vocation. He especially enjoyed admiring (and lamenting) the house he and his wife refinished as well as blaming assorted mishaps on what he called his "CP" leg. He never learned how to properly read analog time or type without watching his fingers.

Victor had an eclectic set of interests including reading the works of G. K. Chesterton and books about the sixteenth-century English Martyrs, collecting novelties from the 1933 World's Fair, and writing postcards to his great-great-aunt Jean. He came up with a brief summary of his life, which reads, "He was lighthearted but intense," which most people who know him well would agree with.

Before listing his survivors and predecessors, he wanted to thank all those who made him into the man he was and who helped him pursue the dreams he had at eighteen years old of marrying his lovely wife and becoming a funeral director; he would also like to thank the DuBores for their outstanding generosity over the years.

He is survived by the one whom he loved above all people, his wife, Paige; sons, Edmund "Ned," Arthur, and Peter; daughter, Fiona Frances; his parents, Bob and Michelle; brothers, Vincent (Kelli) and Bernard (Marissa); grandmothers, MeMe and Gramma KZ; a fair handful of other relatives; way too many cousins; and several close friends and families from Bismarck and Warren.

He was preceded in death by his infant sister, Kathryn Frances; grandparents, Bern and Ruth Sweeney, and Dennis Bolton; several aunts and uncles; great-grandparents, Vic and Ruby; and his dearly loved best friend, Alex.

Please pray for mercy upon his soul.

18

A REQUEST

Any mortician who has been on the job more than a week will hear this following ditty when it comes to discussing funerals: "So, you might think this is strange, but . . ."

This phrase pops up in conversations where one expects it. Anybody approaching sheepishly, with eyes that can't quite meet yours, is likely to soften the blow of their so-called bizarre request before springing it upon you. Odds are it isn't all that strange—a granddaughter asking to rearrange the flowers at the front of the chapel, or a son asking if it's okay if we put slippers on his father's feet instead of the shoes he brought. To me, these requests are fairly typical, even anticipated, and are fairly easy to accommodate.

I suppose this awkwardness when it comes to talking about our desires right before or after a loved one passed is inescapable for most folks (aside from those of us in the death trade). Hardly anybody knows what to say or how to act when the inevitable arrives. Death brings with it a certain sense of decorum that a family feels they must adhere to. To break this decorum, then, is to request something almost impolite, departing from the usual way of things, which might feel "wrong." The lived reality tells me there is no "usual way." Every single funeral diverges from the so-called script because people are unpredictable around the most predictable thing. It is the job of the funeral director in charge to try to accommodate these requests as they arise, sometimes last minute.

This past March, a man died in another state and his cremated remains were shipped home to Minnesota. I met with his mother, Sandy, to complete some paperwork and pin a tentative date for an April burial. With the use of a backhoe, caskets can be buried in the colder months, but an urn requires only a small hole shoveled by hand. It would be impossible to dig through the three-foot-deep ground frost we had this year, and so we'd have to wait until spring.

When his remains arrived to me in the mail, I filled the urn and screwed the threaded top onto the blue brass jar. When Sandy came into the back office to pick it up, she gave me an uncomfortable look and said, "So, you might think this is strange, but . . . ," and then told me she has her son's baby teeth from his tooth fairy days. She read online that all DNA is destroyed in cremation and that we ought to bury some of his DNA with him.

In went the teeth, clinking against the brass as I shook them to the bottom of the urn.

Was it kind of a macabre and strange request? Maybe. But I get why she wanted to do it. To have a proper piece of her son's genetic makeup to keep with her, alongside the rest of him, as she waits for burial. There is a beauty in having mementos from his innocent beginning mixed with the remains of bones that lived in harder years that followed. He is, in some ways, more intact than ever because of his mother's willingness to make what was clearly an uncomfortable, but not unreasonable, request.

There is, however, one wish from years ago that still sticks in my mind as truly strange.

The preface of "So, you might think this is strange, but . . ." really applied for the first time, and I was left with a few questions and, as it turned out, a solution.

———•———

AFTER THE CALL COMES IN, I hop in the car and drive east along Highway 1. Over the bridge and down a gravel road into a thicket of trees, there's a farmhouse with the back light on. It is nighttime, as it always is, it seems, when there's work to be done. As I trundle the cot up the rutted walk to the back door, a sheriff's deputy greets me. Jonny was found by his neighbor this evening. The deputy helps me muscle the cot into the home, and we wind our way through a maze of books and vinyl records to where Jonny is resting at the bottom of the stairs in a body bag, the deputy and the dutiful neighbor already having done the heavy lifting for me. I thank them as we move him to the cot and once more out the door, down the steps, and to my van. I speak with Jonny's siblings despite the hour, and we set a time to meet the day after next to line up his cremation and, as they tell me, no typical service.

In our arrangement, I learn that Jonny was solitary and

softhearted, keeping to his books on the farm and tending the birds he fed and the barn kittens he sheltered. I also learn this salient fact: Jonny loved fireworks.

"So, you might think this is strange, but . . . can we make Jonny into a firework?"

I'm left speechless, which doesn't come easy.

"Um . . . I mean, yes, technically you could." (Wondering quietly why you would want to or whether you even ought to do that.)

"I bet nobody has asked you that before."

"You'd be correct." I laugh. "But actually, I know a guy."

A high school classmate's family owns a fireworks stand in North Dakota. More than a few of my buddies were hired for seasonal jobs during those chaotic weeks around the Fourth of July to sell sparklers and explosives. I place a few calls and talk to the owner himself, Bruce, who also finds this request odd, but nonetheless, he's on board. He gives me the number for his custom guy, Troy, who coincidentally has family living in a nearby town and will be visiting soon.

I make the exchange in a parking lot, suspiciously handing Troy a bag of grey powder. In return, he takes me to the trunk of his car, where he shows me his homemade wares, a hodgepodge of brown-paper-wrapped mortar shells, foil-covered Roman candles, and cartoonish rockets complete with red conical caps. An outlandish request requires an outlandish solution. I point to the one I want.

He'll make Jonny's departure look like something out of a Wile E. Coyote cartoon.

Come April, I meet with Jonny's family in person. Two

dozen cases of last season's fireworks had been donated by Bruce, along with sparklers and fountains galore. He'd told me he couldn't do anything with them anyway, so he was happy to give them away to help clear inventory as well as be a part of something so peculiar. After we load these into the family's truck, I give them Jonny's Rocket and the rest of his bone dust that hadn't fit into what will be the finale of a fireworks show that will happen the first week of May.

Then I call the sheriff's department. The same deputy who helped me with Jonny's body hands me over to the sheriff himself.

"So, you might think this is strange, but . . . I have a favor to ask of you."

And I proceed to tell him the whole story.

He's known Jonny practically his whole life, and his smile is audible over the phone. "I tell you what, Victor. Fireworks aren't allowed to be shot off outside of the Fourth of July and New Year's. But being this is a funeral event, how about the force finds itself needing to be on the *west* side of town that day?"

And so, without any interference, the show goes off without a hitch. It's my night off, and I can't see past the trees in town as I look east to where the fellowship, food, and fireworks are taking place. And I can never be sure if I heard the exact one in the whispering *craack*s that reach me on the front porch. I like to think that last one, the little *pop* I catch on the evening wind, is Jonny's Rocket, sounding softly in the ears of those who knew this quiet man as I did, but loudly in the hearts of those gathered below who knew him best.

19

THE USUAL ATTIRE

I AM WRITING THIS WHILE SITTING in the foyer of North Star Manor, the nursing home here in town. I nod to Phyllis's son as he passes by. Relatives keep arriving to attend her bedside before she's brought into my care, each one walking past giving me a pained smile or a subdued greeting. It might seem ominous, having to make one's way by the mortician and his cot, but I buried Phyllis's husband, Willie, earlier this year and am familiar. I also don't look the part of "undertaker," wearing a band-collar shirt under a fisherman's sweater, khakis, and regularly polished Red Wing boots.

Being unassuming is good: too flashy and you look like you're happy to be there; too somber becomes off-putting and scary. There is some middle way to tread, and it is important when considering clothing, however inscrutable the line is between "respectable" and "approachable."

The selection of clothing is a significant part of the funeral process for those who work in the funeral home, those attending the funeral, and those who are at the center of it all. Wardrobe plays a role in how we adorn, remember, and celebrate our dead.

I'll never forget Great-Grandpa Ralph's tan sport coat that he was buried in. Apart from looking familiar, it made the casket smell like his house—a distinct combination of cigar smoke and baby powder. His funeral was the first I attended after I had committed to pursuing funeral service as a profession. My great-uncle, knowing this, or unwilling to approach the man in charge, requested I place two wood-tipped cigarillos in Ralph's pocket and the glasses on his kindly, wrinkled face. Uncle Danny must have been a little intimidated by the undertaker, standing there in his black suit.

And though I was playing a role many family members have played before, deputized to send grave goods with the dead, it is still the mortician who gets a body mostly ready: embalmed, made up, and dressed. That's not to say a family doesn't still have their part in the process. I like to encourage families when at the bedside to think about bringing a few things to the funeral arrangement meeting we set.

"Please bring a good picture we can use for the obituary. Even though it is hard and I know it has just happened, start thinking about a date and time. And please bring clothing if you're able. It can be something formal or casual. And please include all the usual undergarments."

Sometimes those at the bedside ask about shoes and I respond, "Families bring them in less than half the time. I wouldn't worry about it."

A MONTH AGO I HAD a family bring in shoes for their mother, Irene. Clunky white Velcro sneakers. They brought in all the rest, too. A red blazer, a pair of black slacks, a white turtleneck shirt. The usual raiment of the simple farmwife getting dressed up. The funeral was one that would "follow the script," so to speak, without anything out of the ordinary. We planned it without any trouble. Then, at the end of the arrangements, her daughter asked if she could help get Irene dressed.

This is something we usually undertake alone and in a way that works best with our schedule. The needs of the living have to come before the dead. One can get a body dressed in the middle of the night if push comes to shove. And not too many people ask to help with it; this was the third instance in my career. I told her she could absolutely help and that we'd set up a time.

Irene is now in the front of the funeral chapel on a dressing table, a thick blanket pulled up to her chin. I've put on her undergarments to cover her nakedness before the daughter, Bernie, comes to assist with the rest. Bernie shares that she was an EMT and no stranger to this sort of thing. I'm glad. But I tell her there is also a difference: Irene will be cold to the touch and stiff, the preservatives in the embalming fluid firming her features and muscles into the positions in which I placed them when she was embalmed the night before. Her hands sit over the belly button, with the left over the right, so as to more easily show the wedding ring from 1954 she will wear. Also visible will be incisions in her neck and both thighs, where I gained access to her arteries. These are sutured closed, neither ugly nor pretty, but unusual features on Irene's thin body.

Irene has gone from the flaccidity of death to the stiffness of rigor mortis; from the "breaking" of that rigor by manipulation and a sort of postmortem calisthenics, to again a stiffness caused by embalming.

We each take a position on either side of the table and start by rolling up the blanket and putting on her socks. Then we slide on her slacks, Bernie being directed to reach through the pant leg, grasping her mother's foot as we slide the slacks up her thighs. I roll Irene toward me while the pants come over a buttock, and it is repeated with Bernie rolling her. Now to the shirt.

It is common in funeral service to cut clothing down the back when necessary. Sometimes a shirt is too big or pants are too small. Cutting down the back seam provides the ability to add a pant size or two, or tuck in a shirt that would otherwise billow. There is something slightly less dignified about it, and my preference is to leave at least one layer of clothing intact, even if just an undershirt. For Irene we'll cut as little as possible.

Now having clothes on her lower half, I remove the blanket from her torso. A turtleneck is tricky, so I do cut that—but just the neck, not all the way down. Her arms stiffened, we each reach through the sleeves from the outside, grasping Irene's small and knobby hands, and pull them through, as we did the pants. I tell Bernie to stop before the elbow. Then we each strain Irene's rigid arms up, pulling the half-cut turtleneck over her permed hair and down toward her waist. The red blazer is donned by putting her right arm in first, to the elbow. Then I lift her as high as possible, pulling the jacket through behind her back. Finding the sleeve, I pull her left arm through and then roll her my way so Bernie can pull the blazer up her shoulders, straightening out the lapels once Irene is supine again.

Bernie takes a baggie from her pocket and we pin to those lapels about two dozen pins of various sorts: angels for each of her children, an American flag, a cross, two honorifics from the Polish National Alliance, among others. Bernie has a wistful grin as we do this, making sure each pin is in the "right" place, and finally, she slides on her mother's wedding band. It was awkward coaching an outsider through actions both intimate and yet (to Bernie) unfamiliar. A task that I usually do wordlessly and in half the time. But it is right indeed.

———•———

IN THE NURSING HOME, PHYLLIS'S family is now ready for me. I head down the familiar hallway and enter the familiar room. We talk for a while and I share that she was the sole person to offer me a banana while doing at-home prearrangements and I still think about it. Then the nursing home chaplain speaks up from the hallway and tells us about Phyllis's remarkable generosity. It seems it extended beyond whatever happened to be in reach, to everyone in her last days.

Just yesterday he asked her, "How can I pray for you as the end is near?"

To which she replied, "Don't worry about me. Pray for the staff here, they need it more."

We laugh a little and I see all of us look upon Phyllis warmly as we shroud her in a sheet and pull her to the cot together. We set a time to meet and I give her family the usual words about bringing along an obituary photo and clothing.

The former they'll bring on their cell phones.

The latter is placed immediately in my arms.

A long dress with a shawl, both homemade by a friend.

Clothing to adorn, remember, and celebrate their dead.

20

RECKLESS CHARITY

WHEN IT COMES TO MONEY, I make enough to get all the things I need and most of the things I want. Of course, I try to be conscious of keeping my wants attainable. One way to do that is to not burden myself with worrying too much about the future or the prospects of what "enough" looks like when the future finally arrives. I more or less subscribe to my maternal grandmother MeMe's method of money management, for better or worse.

MeMe lives in a double-wide trailer in my mom's small Michigan hometown. Napoleon is even smaller than Warren, but the trailer park is larger than the one we have here. She lives in the same trailer in which she raised my mother while also taking care of her own parents.

MeMe is something of a character. She has a subtle, almost southern lilt to her voice, and I'm not sure why that is exactly. Michigan is hardly known for its folksy accents, but there's very little more comforting to me now than remembering MeMe asking me as a boy with that twang of hers, "Is we gonna have a good time this weekend, honey?" And I did spend an awful lot of weekends with her.

In addition to caring for her aging parents, MeMe would give my two brothers and me individual "spoil weeks." A spoil week was one in which she would take one of us for an undetermined amount of time and have us follow her around: in the trailer, at work, or with Mom's second cousins and other aged relations. Every evening we would get to stay up late and watch movies with Great-Grandma and Great-Grandpa, finally trudging off to share a bed with MeMe, already asleep in her room with TV fuzz acting as both night-light and white noise machine. A spoil week included ice cream, a reward for kissing our great-grandparents on the cheeks; going to work with MeMe at her window treatment workshop (run out of a defunct church); maybe a trip to the local kite and toy store; with each day bookended by a home-cooked meal prepared by my great-grandmother. Or, we might go out for a meal at the local Big Boy restaurant with its still-intact smoking section. In retrospect, my spoil week consisted of a simple time with a minimal budget. I considered an ice cream cone or bucket of popcorn from the gas station a kingly treat.

As far as how MeMe manages her money, both then and now, the long and short of it is that MeMe still lives in semi-poverty. She is never afraid, though, to spend money on the things that matter. She gives what she has, which often isn't much more than a roof over her head with a little bit left over for groceries. When a young gal in her town fell on hard times,

MeMe put her up in the second bedroom of her trailer rent-free. For five years. My junior year in college, one of her ancient aunts died, leaving each of the nieces and nephews a nice little windfall. MeMe spent her portion on fixing some things in the trailer. After that she gave most of the remaining money to her church and to her friends (including the guy across the street, who would trap all the critters that would move in under the trailer throughout the year). She polished off her inheritance by taking her sister's grandkids on a trip out to North Dakota to see us. Time and money are treated with indifference by my grandma. They all become a gift.

A prudent person might look at the sort of income from her aunt and sock it away for a rainy day or set it aside for paying such frivolous things like taxes and health insurance. MeMe doesn't have much interest in that. Say what you will about my grandma's lack of financial acumen, she knows the value of things that truly matter. And that is priceless.

As to what that means to me, a potential future business owner, I guess we'll see what happens. I want to be successful, but not at the expense of disordered priorities. Unlike MeMe, I will pay my taxes, but I also want to embrace the sort of reckless charity that she embodies.

DEBRA WORKS AT THE DAIRY Queen. In Warren, our Dairy Queen is only open seasonally, during spring and summer. That's part of the cost of living in the far north: nobody wants ice cream when it is minus-twenty degrees out. In any case, when the weather is nice, we take the kids to DQ an awful lot, blowing through our summer treat budget pretty quickly. Debra's smiling face is always at the window or the counter, ready to ask us in her lovely, raspy voice what it is we'd like to order. I, too, have a somewhat distinctive voice up here, lacking the usual long "Minnesota O" that has stubbornly clung on through however many generations since the first Norwegians landed on the prairie. When we talk on the drive-thru intercom we recognize each other's voices right away.

Debra's husband, Sonny, as he was called—a large guy with slicked-back hair and a story always at the ready—had a big personality. Debra met him in unusual circumstances, literally running off with a guy from the circus. He didn't make it easy on her and they lived in a sort of friendly estrangement. When Sonny died a few years ago, Debra and I became close, partly because of her openness in sharing this underlying struggle during our time planning the funeral and subsequent meetings. There was also a financial struggle. These two sorts of hardships often bring people together.

Some families just don't have much. Or what they do have doesn't translate well to paying funeral bills. DuBore's is lucky to have a very good relationship with the county up here when we work to provide a county burial. Marshall County (nine thousand souls and zero traffic lights) is sprawling, but sparse. Much of the population centers around Warren in the southwestern corner of the region. As such, it is where the county courthouse and all the related social services offices are. There is plenty of give-and-take in our relationship with the county. They will advise seniors looking to go on medical assistance to come visit me to preplan their funerals, securing me some future business. We, in turn, provide county burial services, funerals rendered (with an emphasis on simplicity) for those of limited means, at the stipend they set for us. We always lose money on the deal, but it is well worth doing. Some of the finest people I have met in our area have availed themselves of these services. And these families who are being served by a small government subsidy and our charity are often the most grateful. There is still a financial transaction taking place, but it's behind the scenes, not requested from the family, but from social services, and is minimal. This is part of the reason why I don't like taking payment for funerals up front if I can help it. I want my work to have its basis in charity. That I get paid to do it is a nice bonus and keeps me able to do it for others, but I never want it to become the goal of my work.

The stark reality is that an exchange still must take place. You give me several thousands of dollars and your dead. In return I'll handle the ins and outs of their death. For my daily bread, I'll pick up your dead loved one in my arms at the nursing home and lay them on my cot. To make ends meet, I'll file death certificates, disposition permits, help navigate life insurance benefits, or submit veteran's paperwork for your newly deceased. My time, whether in my office, the embalming room, or in my bed soon to be awoken, becomes yours.

Debra and I worked with the county to provide burial for Sonny, and while the funeral home worked for free and part of the bill was paid by the social services office at the courthouse, there were still some expenses left over, namely a headstone. Despite some reservations, Debra plans to be buried next to

Sonny. Her philosophy is "Well, I lived with him this long, what else is new?"

Every person has their path in life, and more than a few of us are accompanied along the way by people who bring us equal parts joy and trouble. That's part of life. Debra could teach a master class on it, she tolerates life so well. With this in mind, it seemed fitting that for Debra and Sonny's headstone, they share a marker while still having some separation. They each kept their marriage vows and I think that is something to be celebrated, however it turned out in the end. Her toleration in life will have some physical recognition in death. For their stone I created a design featuring two halves. His name on the left (next to his brother's cemetery lot) and hers on the right, with a line that runs smack down the middle. Her side has a maiden name listed: a sort of biographical detail that speaks to her roots while also giving Debra a connection to family that isn't solely through her up-and-down marriage. The design looks pretty classic and tells a story if you know where to look.

Debra told me she wanted something nice, even if it would be hard to finance, as money was tight. The subtext is that she didn't want a less-expensive flat marker, something to get lost in the almost ever-present snow up here. In that cemetery, too, most of the stones are upright. She has "neighbors" and didn't want them to think she went with the cheaper option. I told her I'd figure it out—the stone, the money, the neighbor issue. In a stroke of luck, my granite shop bought a competitor that same year and it came with a scrap pile, odds and ends of stone that sat in a back lot collecting dust. After getting permission, I went on a hunt to find Debra and Sonny something nice.

In the hodgepodge of chipped granite, stained marble bevels, and misprinted veterans' markers sat Debra's stone. It is three feet long, two feet tall, polished on the sides and top, and is an odd color. My granite guys weren't even sure from what quarry it originated and, upon doing some follow-up, told me that the previous owner wasn't sure, either. It came with the business when he bought it decades before. What looked like a misfit to them was to me an opportunity.

I got it for a song. A piece of granite nobody would use was free: Debra would only pay for labor. The design I already had in my mind, but it came with another little hurdle: the stone was just the top of a headstone—there was no base associated with it. Taking a cue from the monoliths of the last century, I had the illusion of "feet" engraved into the edges. It appears to flare at the bottom and, looking as if it has a base, draws the eye upward to create something of the illusion of the height of its neighbors.

Debra tacitly approved the design, trusting me to carry out her plan: create something nice and don't break the bank. When it came time to pay, even what seems nominal for a headstone was more than she could cover, what with disposing of what was left of Sonny's things, moving from her apartment into his house, and trying to find help to replace the things in the home he'd long neglected.

For a year, each time we would visit DQ, Debra would slip me some cash to put toward the stone. Then last year the cash-to-headstone pipeline slowed down as the repairs on the home grew more onerous. Leaking windows and pipes put an end to our unspoken agreement and cash exchanges. So, I paid off the balance myself. Debra is a friend, not just a customer, and a few hundred dollars is well worth the service we get from her all summer long—especially when I bring four rambunctious kids to drip ice cream all over the restaurant. Truth be told, I probably give away what I paid on the headstone in Dairy Queen tips every year.

This is the kind of MeMe-an reckless charity I strive for. Say what you will about good business practices and responsible annual budgeting, I believe that my return on (human) investment will yield far more than anything you could find on a profit-and-loss statement.

21

STRICTLY BUSINESS

BUT WHAT OF THE FUNERAL home as a business? It is taking me quite a while to come to terms with that, as I entered the profession a starry-eyed dreamer pretty much ignorant of the commercial side of things. As I have acquired and grown my rather peculiar skill set, it has become clear to me that the abilities I have are able to support a business and are probably worth paying for.

For one, they're not that common. There's something like thirty thousand funeral directors working in the country today. That's about one for every eleven thousand people. This is skewed by situations like mine, where we have three licensed morticians working in the same small town, at the same funeral home. But this understanding of the mortuary as a business has grown alongside my recognition of the value of my work and its odd place in the fabric of life. Do I particularly like charging money to show up at a home and bring a dead body into my care? Not really. It is sometimes rather hard, but also beautiful, and that is where I find it valuable. I get so much from the family (trust or appreciation) in exchange for the unusual (but commonplace to me) action of bearing their dead to my workplace.

I do much of my job, exercising this hard-earned (and sometimes hard-maintained) skill set, for love.

The classic definition of "Love" is "to will the good of another." Basically, if you and I can want what is good for the other, whatever that might look like, and then try to procure it, we're in love! It might sound strange coming from the guy who says he'll love you by sewing up Mom's incisions or flushing out her bowels, but there it is. I wouldn't do these things for any other reason; money isn't enough of a motivator to complete these morbid tasks. Truly, I want to learn to love every family I serve, providing a particular kind of charity that comes with walking into dark situations.

"I DON'T KNOW WHAT TO do. Help."

These words or something similar were part of my first interaction with Lori Greentree. They stick out in my mind not because they were unusual. Families do not generally know what to do when loss comes. Death brings with it a sort of paralysis; the next step is always somewhat hesitant and in the dark. The funeral business thrives on knowing a little of the unknown.

Lori's call from an out-of-state number comes to me out of the blue. Working at the funeral home, we don't get the luxury of avoiding unwanted spam calls. For as many robocalls as we field, we get an equal number of people asking from a distance questions about funeral times or flowers. In Lori's case, she calls with bad news that would begin a couple weeks of hard days—and some good days that followed. It oftentimes happens like that.

I ask how I can help and begin to feel out the details. Mom and Dad are dead. Spouses don't usually go together, so that's surprising.

Where? *Michigan in some county or other.*
When? *I only just found out.*
How? *A car crash. A fiery one.*

Her parents were driving across Michigan and got into a wreck, one so bad the car burst into flames. She doesn't know too much more apart from the basic facts. I reassure her I'll find out what to do next, take down her number, and do an internet search to direct me to the county coroner where the crash happened. It is helpful to have someone to talk to the deathcare workers on the other end. They can describe the situation with a frankness that exists between professionals in the field. No words need to be softened, no turns of phrase checked. The medical examiner tells me that Charles and Maureen were removed from the wreck, but not before their bodies were entirely consumed by fire. The folks on the scene were thorough. All human remains were divided into two separate body bags. They inventoried what non-remains they could, and it amounts to some metal (probably the remnants of a past surgery), a bracelet, and two wedding bands.

I've had a few accidents ending in fire in my career thus far and the results are always profoundly horrific. Depending on the situation, bodies appear shrunken or blackened, with limbs retracted into odd and unnatural positions.

I relay the difficult news to Lori. This, too, is part of the business. One has to be sensitive, but also realistic. You tell a family the hard facts, but gently, with what love you can.

"Lori, I finished talking with the medical examiner. She told me that there is nothing left to view of Mom and Dad. The fire . . ."

I don't finish the sentence and am met with prolonged silence on the other end.

"In a case like this, there is only one decision to make. . . . Would you like to bring what (little) remains home in a shared casket, or would you rather we . . . let the fire complete what it started?"

"Victor, I don't . . ."

We share a silence.

"There's no easy way to do it, Lori, but I'll do whatever I can, one step at a time after that, okay?"

As we work our way through the process, having the family sign off on documents and transfers for cremation in Michigan, I help them figure out those next steps. The USPS does indeed deliver her parents' remains to me in standard shipping urns. Nestled in each one is a wedding ring, rubber-banded to the bag of cremated remains. We plan a funeral long-distance. I write a joint obituary for the joint service. Lori and I exchange emails and texts as we finalize the date for what will be a graveside service in the little country churchyard, where the late happy couple were married almost five decades prior.

Before Lori comes to town, I must finalize one last thing.

A jeweler I know has stayed open past closing time so I can deliver a small pouch containing something more precious than most other gold and gemstones in the store.

I hand him two blackened rings of bent metal along with the twisted and charred links of chain.

When Lori arrives in Warren a day before the funeral, I tell her I have something for her. That, in addition to the usual handling of people, places, and things related to the funeral, I called in a favor so something good might come of the tragedy she has endured. Burying both of your parents on the same day brings with it few consolations. Here was one I could procure.

I hand her a jewelry case. She opens it. On a pillow sit two gleaming gold bands. A bracelet encircles the two, completing the presentation of the only things to survive the car crash apart from her parents' bone dust remains, now safely enclosed in a shared urn. Crying happens. For us both. I, too, have had tough days lining up the details of every child's worst nightmare.

Shared tears feel good.

Lori and her family meet at the church the following day. The minister I recommended to Lori shares some stories from the family along with a message of hope and encouragement. We set her mom and dad gently into the earth. Two men in dress blues fold and present a burial flag for her dad. The trumpeting of taps begins and fades away into the chilly springtime air that stirs the new crops just coming up in the field across the way. We head inside and eat, grateful for warm food. I receive a hug and then depart, having made a friend. I notice two gold rings on a chain around Lori's neck.

That summer Lori calls me again. Not in a panic this time. She's got good news: she's getting married.

She needs my help again.

The little country church of her parents' wedding will be the same venue for her own. As it turns out, I do, in fact, know where to get food and, yes, I'll have the same presiding minister line up a Zoom call for some premarriage meetings.

I order her wedding bouquet to match the one her mother held in 1974. And I tell our florist to send me the bill.

It is more than just business. It always has been.

It is love.

22

THE PRICE WE PAY FOR LOVE

IF YOU HAPPEN TO NEED my expertise there's a good chance I'll see you naked. Like the local doctor or dermatologist, I've seen my fair share of naked bodies while honing and practicing this peculiar skill set.

Like most professionals who work in medicine-adjacent fields, I see the human body, while still being wonderfully made and mysterious in its workings, through a scientific lens. There is a sort of strange intimacy with the human body that morticians share with surgeons and dentists. I'm not too fazed by seeing someone's grandmother sans clothing. I've seen hundreds of naked little old ladies and little old men and I'm here to tell you—they are all very much the same. Limbs, torso, and a single head. There are obviously various sexual characteristics, but these don't really change the work much: a penis may have to be tied off to prevent leaking, or a set of breasts "lifted" by a clever little corset stitch between them, but mostly, the bulk of the bodywork has to do with the things we all have in common.

As much as I say I have a somewhat scientific view of the body, I suppose that the lens only extends to when I am actively working on one. Most of the time, the body is seen as much more than a systematic vehicle composed of various tissues and fluids. I like the fact that we all have this body in common. One can see snatches of oneself in everyone else. It's easy for me to see that these bodies tend to wear out. I find my own is doing the same despite it only operating for a short thirty-some years. I was born premature and with cerebral palsy. Much of my childhood was spent in physical therapy learning how to walk with one good leg and one short "CP" one that didn't flex too much. My drop foot was operated on and my Achilles tendon was cut and spliced, giving me a better range of motion, though I still walk with a limp. It was only a few years ago that the childhood mantra that my father drilled into me of "heel-toe, heel-toe" has faded into my subconscious. But the bad leg is needing more maintenance as I, too, start to wear out. I can't help but empathize with the bodies that come through my door.

But even as I limp daily toward middle age, I recognize that I am luckier than many. At the very least I have my mind. It's a common sentiment heard around the funeral home. Things like "Well, at least he had his wits about him until the end," despite lying in bed for half a decade. Or on the contrary, "It's almost like she died years ago," when talking to a family whose mother began her descent into Alzheimer's early on.

Now, some might see this idea of physical or mental degradation becoming a burden to ourselves or the ones we love.

And feeling you'll be a burden someday is a burden in and of itself. It's often enough that people change their funeral plans so as to "not be a burden."

To this I say, "Be a burden. It's your last chance!"

ROGER HAS DIED. HIS PLANS are all written out just as he wanted them. We are to have a funeral in the Lutheran church with his body there. As something of a pillar of the satellite community of Radium, he has accounted for this and has made sure his obsequies are up to his state in life: a well-liked, known figure about town and donor to many organizations and projects. In his file we have his obituary, a notation of where memorials might be sent in his memory, and his casket selection. Everything is preplanned and paid for. All that is left is to meet with his wife and family to pick a date and time.

His wife, Darlene, arrives with their three children, all of whom are already grandparents themselves. Roger has lived to ninety-two and is a patriarch. He will be celebrated in death the way he envisioned. I have his file at the ready and have priced everything out for the funeral arrangement. Our meeting should take half the time of a typical funeral arrangement where all details and choices need to still be decided.

And then Darlene drops the bomb. Roger has become terribly inconvenient in his death. In fact, he has been especially inconvenient this last week in the hospital, and damn it all, things are "too puffed up" around funerals, she tells me.

Too many nice things said, too many flowers, too much money "wasted." Darlene dictates that Roger should be cremated with just a simple visitation at the funeral home. Nobody cares, nobody will remember him, and whatever plans he made are just "too much."

This funeral arrangement will not be a quick one.

Darlene picks apart every decision on file (much of it hand-written by Roger himself) and contradicts everything that had been planned based upon her husband's directives. No, we won't have the Lutheran minister, even just to close us in a prayer. No, sharing some memories would be too much trouble. No, the grandkids won't want to see him. One small victory is found by including a little scribble we would make, his monogram if you will, in a funeral program being put together along with his obituary. She concedes that people might want to take something home to remember him by—but she won't be fooled into paying for a meal or refreshment for anyone who comes through to pay their respects.

As the adult children silently go along with this, I watch Roger's legacy unravel. The accomplishments are listed with gusto in the obituary, but no thought is given to people who might come to acknowledge them. Half of Radium is in his debt in one way or another. Yet Darlene claims time and time again that nobody will actually care.

Six days later, on a Thursday evening, three hundred people walk through the doors of DuBore's to say goodbye to Roger. Maybe it is a small-town thing, but I get cornered dozens of times with people asking me under their breath, "Where is he?" We didn't even put an urn up front, per Darlene's specifications.

Church members scratch their heads, coworkers and board members ask me what time the funeral will be the next day. I hardly know how to answer. The reply "We had to change some plans" satisfies nobody, but at least it is a true, if incomplete, description of what happened.

It was reassuring, despite the sad circumstances, to see tangible proof that we are not inconveniences, but something more.

CAN WE BE INCONVENIENT? SURE. Try moving a dead body sometime. Each one is either too tall, too fat, or too fragile. We're a lot of work, even when we're dead. I've cradled a lady of 65 pounds in my arms like a child, her daughter watching me lift her from the leather sectional on which she died; I've deadlifted 450-pound men with the help of a single sheriff's deputy; and bent the knees of fellas over six foot five up to incredible heights to get them to fit on my cot. (Feet hanging out of the end of a body bag is not a good look, nor does it make for great optics when the cot pouch won't close over toes or someone's immense stomach.)

But as inconvenient as it is to manipulate the dead and drag their weight at their life's end, I like to remember that this is par for the course when it comes to being human. For as much as we change, in some respects we never do. We're made to be inconvenient from the very beginning. We enter this world naked, not knowing what we're about. And shortly after we end this life, we're again naked on a mortuary table or shrouded in a bedsheet in a cremate-able box, far beyond knowing anything at all. Mixed in with all the wonder and magic we each bring to life, there are some challenges we dole out all the same; even from the time we are conceived we oftentimes make our mothers ill with morning sickness and put a tremendous physical toll on them. Then we become children and make our parents' hair turn grey and the lines on their faces deepen. We go off on our own, and little changes, except that our decisions are now magnified. We often make the wrong ones. In addition to creating conflicts inside our very selves, we cause anxiety in others from the sheer fact we exist.

It has been said that "tears are the price we pay for love." I propose another axiom: "Inconvenience is the price we pay for love." It's less catchy an epitaph or condolence written in a sympathy card, but it is certainly true. Possibly truer, as we're inconvenient for a far longer time than we cry over a death. We cry for a while, but inconvenience lasts forever (another nice epitaph, maybe).

And it's somewhat ironic, in that I think we truly excel at inconvenience when we try to avoid it. There is an ancient fable that has been told and reported in many ways, but is familiar to me through the pen of W. Somerset Maugham. In "The Appointment in Samarra," a merchant assists his servant in fleeing down the road from Death, who was just glimpsed across their Baghdad marketplace, to the eponymous town. Death is scolded by the merchant for startling his hired man and Death replies he was startled, too: he wasn't expecting the servant to be in Baghdad. He had an appointment with him that night in Samarra. We meet the thing we set out to avoid and in our changing of plans come face-to-face with the very thing we fear.

And Darlene was fleeing down that road with the servant.

For every way the plan diverged from what Roger explicitly wanted, some new problem was created. Instead of burying him in the ground we now had to discuss what to do with his cremated remains. And instead of having his friends listed as casket bearers, I'd have to wrangle them up ad hoc as we went about a two-hour open visitation with attendees in flux, trying to tell them that Roger would have honored them . . . if we were honoring Roger in the ways he clearly outlined. It was more than awkward. Nobody was satisfied. Thank God Roger wasn't around to see the mess that was made.

When it comes to inconvenience, a balance should be struck that honors the dead while also serving the living. When I am dead, I want to make some things easier, if I can. The hard parts cannot be avoided, though; the transportation and preparation of my body, the gathering of family from wherever they may be, and organizing the ritual I'd like to have as part of my final goodbye when my time is up. These things will all take sacrifice and love from my family and friends. Some of them will have to take time away from work or their own families. If I die before my wife, I will make her life incredibly inconvenient. This is the price she pays for loving me.

As one who has a very beloved now-dead best friend, I've learned a lot about inconvenience and how to accept it. For one, Alex was inconvenient to have as a friend while living. He was always up to something—probably dangerous, usually foolish, and sometimes illegal. The anxiety I had while he was alive was almost constant. But even now, as the years have continued to flow ever onward past his lifetime, I find that he is still inconvenient, just in a different way.

A great humanity exists apart from and greater than ours, onto which we all are grafted. As a result, familiar traits within it can be seen between wildly different people. Though Alex is unique and wholly original, he is still alive (in a way) when I see him in the faces of others. Two years ago, I saw him in the next town over, standing on the corner by the Walmart, begging for money. I don't know how to explain it exactly, but the man who looked into my car window and said, "Anything helps," was Alex. Dumbstruck, I gave him the few dollars that I had in my wallet. I then drove to the nearest gas station, got some food and a hot coffee and a few twenty-dollar bills, and went back to find this man.

Reggie did not see it as strange at all. When I returned with his food and money, I told him that I saw my dead friend in him: part of Alex was living through him. We shared a smoke and Reggie then told me about his life and struggles. I gave him the scarf from around my neck to bolster him in the cold, as he had only two layers of hoodies to keep him warm. I shook his hand and then we hugged. We hugged a few times more and we each let a few tears fall. It was an odd moment for an outsider to view, a man in a wool overcoat and porkpie hat hugging like a brother a man who was without a home or means. But I knew some part of Alex that I recognized on a subliminal level was crushing my ribs right back. This cosmic humanity we share had come down for a moment and brought me comfort.

And I have seen Alex since. I have seen him in shaking a hand that is smaller, firmer, and rounder than my own. I have seen him in anyone who laughs red-faced and chaotically, or in the young man slouching in the alley next to the convenience store. I once saw Alex in a dad waiting at our daughters' gymnastics class and had to literally sit down. There was something about the shape of his face and his demeanor that made me stop and watch him interact with his daughter, seeing in her the daughter that Alex would never have. It's possible that it is all the product of an imagination run wild, but I like to think that humanity recognizes humanity—especially when it recognizes it with love.

Is it convenient, being unexpectedly taken aback and unable to watch my daughter's wily gymnastic tumbles? Is it convenient, still keeping a spare set of winter boots in the back of my van in case I run into Reggie again? These things are inconvenient, and that's okay. It's one more burden to add to the pile that we take on as living, breathing parts of humanity. It is a burden we bear because we have loved.

I will be just as inconvenient to my children when I am dead as they are to me while I am living. So why shy away from this final inconvenience? I hope my family and friends love me enough to accept my inconvenience, my ungainly corpse, and the interruptive time of my funeral rites. But I also love them enough to know that they can make my inconveniences and plans work for them, too. At least a little bit.

It is okay to be inconvenient to your loved ones. If it is a thing we all share, then it is mutual. We're inconvenient coming and going.

DARLENE DIED TODAY.

Who knows what her family will ask for when they arrive at arrangements, but not much of her family joins me in making them. As it turns out, not all the children show up like they did for their dad. Maybe they feel that the one person present to make the decisions is enough. It turns out they'd talked it over beforehand. They learned a lesson last time they sat around this table, and not necessarily a good one. Mom valued convenience.

"Victor, just burn her up and hand her over," the lone child quips.

And so, I do just that. They write an obituary without my input. I place her emaciated body in a cardboard cremation container and drive her to the crematory. Someone from the family will pick her up when she's done. They're going to host their own funeral across town, I'm told. I only provide exactly what they ask for; they require neither sundries nor suggestions.

A few months pass and still no funeral has materialized. It can only happen, I presume, at a convenient time for everyone. When it finally happens, I hear it is a subdued affair. A walk into a public building with her picture on display. They've buried her at some other time in some other place. In the intervening months, though, we hear that the family has labored to pull together a picture video; squabbled about where and how to present the obituary; gone back and forth over the location; and they've hashed and rehashed and hashed again everything to the point that most of the decision-makers walked away and left it to a few remaining hardy souls with more patience. It was an inconvenient affair through and through.

Inconvenience is the price we pay for love. It is inevitable. Why try to avoid it?

WHEN I LOOK BACK ON the lessons that carry the most weight, it seems that works of fiction are always behind them. Novels and short stories have always driven my capacity for sympathy or tolerance, allowing me to step into the shoes of someone else and become them for as long as the story takes to read or hear. This lesson of accepting inconvenience has been pivotal in my life, creating a view of the aged, infirm, and dying that I hope humanizes them instead of presenting them as a burden. And to tell a fictional story might bring the point home. I am no short story writer and barely an author, so please indulge me as I tell you a fable of my own invention. . . .

To a woman it was foretold that one day she would die and Inconvenience would be there to meet her.

From the time of her birth, Inconvenience had already been following her, stalking her every interaction, a specter in a long cloak who was always just out of sight and yet had his meddling finger in most of her doings. As a baby, the woman was cradled to sleep by Inconvenience. Her mother and father welcomed him into their home, knowing that he would live with them for as long as their beautiful daughter did. And when she moved out, the Shade's brother, Anxiety, would take up residence. This did not surprise them. They loved their daughter and accepted these houseguests as a condition of the joys they would feel as they watched her grow.

But as she grew, the young girl, now ever approaching womanhood, saw Inconvenience when she looked in the mirror. She did all she could to avoid his grasp. She tried doing everything herself, pushing away others offering her aid, not in agreement with those so willing to court Inconvenience when she herself knew better: Inconvenience was a menace, something that would make her weak. She would not let the premonition come true. She would be the one to cheat Inconvenience, if ever anyone could.

She had told her loved ones again and again, "Don't trouble with me when I am gone," so often that they forgot that Inconvenience had quietly lurked in the background of their lives spent with her. The Shade had power she knew not.

In her final moment, the woman, after a life spent in fear of Inconvenience, saw her life leave her body as if from above. And she watched Inconvenience drift in and take up residence in her flesh, where once she had control.

And as she looked down into her body's unseeing eyes, she saw a spark that was invisible to the undertaker attending her deathbed (she did not want her family to be called when she passed, for fear that Inconvenience might appear in their midst). He could not see it, but she did. Inconvenience was not only inside of her lifeless remains but was growing in the minds and hearts of all *who knew her. As insubstantially as he drifted in, his smokelike shadow also drifted out to find her loved ones, with little regard for the control she tried to exert over him all these years.*

And then she learned:

There is no control. Inconvenience cannot be outwitted, outsmarted, or otherwise outmaneuvered. Any attempt at love calls him forth, and nobody is free of Inconvenience until the last remnant of their memory has left the minds of men.

23

IN LIVING MEMORY

TO SOME, THE PAUPER'S FIELD of old is a sad place where bodies with nowhere to go were dumped without much care. In Warren, when we have an indigent die, as sometimes happens, there isn't a set place for their body to rest. Rather, they get interred alongside the other residents of town in a cemetery lot donated by the city, if in Greenwood Cemetery, or the Catholic church, if in Calvary Cemetery. Cemetery lots are dirt cheap in either one, having only recently increased to $300 apiece. When I got here it was $150 to own a plot of land four feet wide by eight feet long; the depth is variable depending on what you bury in it. For reference, lots cost four figures in larger towns, and five figures in metropolitan areas.

I own a lot in the Catholic cemetery. I purchased a singleton as insurance I'd stay on the cemetery board when I changed to a more traditional parish. I live within the bounds of Warren, so I suppose I have rights as a coreligionist anyway, but it seemed sensible to be well propertied. And at $150 it was a steal. I don't have plans to use it, and because I'm the sexton, a piece of ground that is taken up by a very conspicuous tree now has my name on it.

As a mortician, one becomes a bit of a realist. There is a folder bearing my name in the file cabinet at DuBore's, detailing my wishes if I die an untimely death. It also lists various accounts, passwords, and where my tax documents are kept in the funeral home's attic.

Thankfully, the cemetery lot has not come into use. At least not for human remains. Our family has buried broken religious goods like rosaries there (as, according to our beliefs, blessed items cannot be discarded and thrown in the trash). I've also begun to dig some of my handcrafts into the turf, mostly for lack of a better place to put them. After coming up with designs for headstones for a number of years, it seemed time to learn how to do some actual carving. I bought a set of hard-stone hand chisels, procured rocks when available, and have gotten to work.

The typical medium of a mortician is dead human flesh. And while this has its value, it is something rather impermanent. We give a body back to a family for a time, then it is either burned up or closed in a box and covered with earth. The ephemeral nature of the thing is good and gives the work of embalming and presentation of the dead meaning at the time it is most needed. But that it is temporary means it disappears when the work is done. The value of body preparation is felt in the mind or the memory once the material of it is out of sight, and the memories can last a lifetime if the job is done right.

An engraved stone can weather hundreds of years or more in the open and lasts visibly much longer than a body, whether in a box or reduced to fit in an urn. I thought this hobby would be a fitting way to complement the very temporary nature of my primary work with bodies and families that come and go.

After receiving my beginner's set of lettering chisels from Trow & Holden, a stone-carving-tool company based in Vermont, I set an ambitious goal: I want to mark all the paupers' graves in the Catholic cemetery. A stone in a cemetery, whether carved by my imprecise hand or another, will last far longer as a testament to the life lived, even of one utterly forgotten, than the body that is now resting, nigh unidentifiable, beneath the turf.

———•———

THE MAPS ON HAND OF Calvary Cemetery and the records kept in Latin at the church office tell me that there are a total of five unmarked graves. A little more research tells me that they are all men, all unmarried, and all farmers. The supporting details are gleaned from the funeral record archives in my office. It might be just a coincidence, but each man is also a first-generation American, immigrating here from somewhere else. Three Poles, a German, and a Mexican occupy the graves that need marking.

There are two things standing in the way of making memorials for each of the identified, but un-memorialized, men. My own skill is a given: I don't know how to do this and have nobody to act as teacher. For the most part, the art of hand-engraving was abandoned with the advent of the power saw and pneumatic chisel. The owners of the monument company I use, operating with technologies unavailable in my run-down, makeshift garage workshop, suggest lots of practice and starting with soft stone, working up to the harder granite. The other obstacle is the lack of funds. I did not have an extra few thousand to spend on each suitable monument for five long-dead men. The budget option of manual labor and scavenged rock will have to do.

On the plus side, anything that comes out of my garage workshop will be substantially better than what exists now—which is nothing. Another advantage is that whatever is put on the grave, no matter how cobbled together or folk art–esque, will receive neither any complaints nor real criticism. Each man died childless decades ago. The earliest burial (1949) and the most recent (1970) have been in graves unmarked for one to two generations.

The suggestion to begin with soft stone is a good one. Working in limestone is like chiseling through frozen butter: it almost crumbles away as the chisel chases lines down the stone. As a preliminary project, I make a panel in limestone cheekily titled *All Flesh Is Grass*, complete with the outline of a skeleton lying beneath some grass and flowers. It goes in the sod of my cemetery lot. After a few more small projects and much "tinkering," which is an onomatopoetic name for the light and repetitive hammering of steel on steel on stone, I scrounge a slightly damaged marble marker from my headstone guys. Harder than limestone, but still less adamantine than granite, this piece is slated for Joseph Miskojeski, buried 1949.

I happily tinker on the marble, fifteen minutes at a pop (usually, all the time I can spare) over the next several months.

I engrave that he was born in Poland and died in the US. A friend of mine who speaks Polish translates "Have mercy on us"; these words, unreadable to me even as I carve them, go on the stone above Miskojeski's name and dates. When I finish, while I'm not totally satisfied with the workmanship, I keep the idea of "something is better than nothing" ever in my mind. I can't let perfection be the enemy of the good here.

Once I haul the marble out to Miskojeski's lot in Calvary, denoted by the sunken ground over his collapsed casket and rough box that held the dirt up (until it didn't, as it is not a vault), I call my friend Chris to lend a hand with the next step.

Chris is the lawyer in town and was recently elected the county attorney. Unassuming and mild-mannered, Chris is something of a mountain man at heart, enjoying time in the woods and working with his hands. He looks like his grandfather Sylvester, whom I knew in his old age, but who in his prime was lean, red-bearded, with an aquiline nose, just like Chris. I ask for his help digging a hole in the cemetery, and without any hesitation or further question, he agrees. Working in the dirt is a noble and needed pastime for two professionals who are kept in the office all too often. In about an hour, we take off the sod, pack the earth, square the corners, and dig in a cement slab as a foundation, placing Miskojeski's new handcrafted marble headstone on top. Chris brushes the stray grass and dirt away from the now-less-forgotten name as I haul off the excess dirt.

Joseph Miskojeski, a pauper, a farmer, and a Pole, has left living memory. All that remains is his name; and not even that until recently.

Living memory is one of those topics I come back to often.

At heart, it is about brevity. Lives seem long when one is living his or her own, grinding out twenty-four hours and doing it again and again until the last day. But when looked at from a distance, living memory, that time when you and I are "known" by those who have come after us, lasts maybe a century after our deaths. Miskojeski has been in the ground for three quarters of a century at this point and hasn't been "known" for ages. Chuck DuBore has been in town longer than practically anyone, and he missed knowing Joseph by a decade.

Even if one is well-known and well-loved, there will come a point when there is nobody alive anymore who knew them. Yes, we know about people like Abraham Lincoln from history books, and we might even know something of their character by their legacy or collected writings. If bold, one might even predict what he or she might think about a current topic with some accuracy, but one can't be sure: they're not around to ask. And while many of us feel we know Lincoln well, the last person to possibly "know" him (at best) died in the 1940s. This person might have told stories of Lincoln or, like a woman buried in Greenwood Cemetery, might have shaken his hand—the fact engraved into her headstone for posterity to read—but true knowledge of the man is long since gone.

Chris and I met a few years ago at his grandpa Sylvester's funeral. He was a man I knew well and cherished. Despite having love of Syl in common, we didn't start hanging out in earnest until a few years ago, despite Chris having come back to work in his local law office a few years before that. When one of you handles the dead bodies and the other their estates, your worlds overlap. It also helps that we were two professional men of the same age in a small town. Nowadays, he and his wife will stop for dinner from time to time and I am just as likely to ask for his help in some oddball task (like unmarked-grave work) as he is to invite me for a drink in his garage to decompress after a long week. He owns some land up north and we've gone out there a few times. He has ambitions to erect a log cabin and showed me the site. The foundation stones are already in the ground and level, salvaged hand-hewn blocks from a building that was demolished and will leave living memory soon enough.

Off to the side of this foundation, however, is a magnificent six-foot-high stone slab leaning against a falling-down shed and various farm debris from decades past. I ask him what it is. "Oh, that? It's my headstone." The slab is reddish sandstone that must have at one time been a threshold or lintel.

"I'd like for you to carve it for me when my time comes."

"Well, sure. But as you know, Chris, I'm fairly terrible at it."

"Well, get to work! You'll have it figured out before I'm under it."

I hope it is the case.

For one thing, the stone is attractive. It is a rock of rich color and texture and is an absolute monolith. It'd be an honor to carve the thing and leave a lasting mark upon its surface. I also know the setting where it will eventually be placed: the country cemetery in the woods abutting Chris's land. The last burial there was sometime in the 1980s and I don't reckon it'll receive another body until Chris, or his wife, lies beneath the stone there.

Sylvester lies beneath a stone, alongside his wife, in Calvary Cemetery. Syl was one of the holiest men I've had the privilege to meet, and I get to think about him often and fondly as I drive by the cemetery or do work there. He comes to mind even more regularly now that I see Chris often and think of *him* fondly. The lines are blurred, both men visible at once, one young and one old. Syl will be in living memory for a while and in mine for as long as it lasts. Chris stands a good chance of making a hundred years "known," as he is around my children an awful lot. My youngest, Peter, asks for him by name in short, toddler-composed sentences, and the middle boy, Arthur, recently told me that Chris is his "oldest friend." In age, that is.

It is said that death is the "great equalizer," and it seems that living memory, being an effect of death, follows the same rules. As much as we're able, I think we all desire to be "known," and to have someone know a few things about us handed down in stories over the decades.

I wish I knew more about Mr. Miskojeski. A glimpse into his life would have made carving his stone come alive in a certain way. But I do know that having his name visible is something, however imperfect.

I hope to someday imperfectly carve Chris's name and his wife's into the stone on his land. And to finish the cemetery markers for the remaining four unmarked graves in my cemetery. But nothing is a guarantee. Except I do know that even if I were to die tomorrow, I could be remembered for almost a century by those left behind. And even when those who remember me are gone and living memory is no more, something else will remain behind in Calvary Cemetery. Not with my name on it, but with Miskojeski's.

24

OPEN TO LIFE, OPEN TO DEATH

I HAVE SERVED THE PRZYBYLSKI FAMILY too many times in my decade in Warren. It started my second year here when we buried Jake. Jake died in a car crash, leaving behind his parents, two siblings, and a son. When a ninety-five-year-old leaves this life, it is almost something we can celebrate. But looking backward over a mere thirty years of life is too short and too painful.

How do we have a "celebration of life" when the life is one-third of what we feel and expect it ought to be? The truth of it is we rarely do.

In situations like these, as a youngish man myself, it is hard not to see myself in the empty spot that is left when another young man dies. Like a cartoon in which a character bursts through a wall leaving their exact outline in the bricks, I would fit into that silhouette all too well. Mark, Jake's dad, would fit the silhouette almost perfectly. He has the same build, maybe slightly taller, and his blond, going-white mustache would make little impact in the outline. During our days together, he told me he'd trade places with his son in a minute.

The sad thing is that Mark could never make that trade, and soon enough had the chip he was so willing to offer taken from him. Just shy of three years after his son's death, Mark, not yet sixty, died unexpectedly of a heart attack.

We once again gathered to mourn the loss of someone gone too soon, knowing he could have had so many more years.

His wife, Brenda, having now buried a son and a husband, relies on her daughter, Tasha, to carry the load for the family in this difficult time. Brenda also has another son, Zach, who is a quadriplegic. Brenda had also lost a baby, Tiffany, back when the family was starting to grow. What was once six, and then for decades five, has now come to three in the matter of a few years, the family now cut in half.

IF I INHABIT A WORLD between the living and the dead, I do so by way of my exposure to the dead and to the bereaved. Tasha enters by my way as well, having half of her immediate family come through my building over the course of a decade. But since this place is the intersection of the living and the dead—can't we also enter it by way of the living?

Life is so very uncertain. Yes, sometimes it ends in a swift death, but often enough each one of us wakes anticipating that we'll close our eyes at the end of the day having accomplished something and having seen a brand-new day from start to finish.

We expect every day to be a little different from the last and not quite know what it holds. I suppose we also accept that the day may or may not go our way, but we'll muddle through all the same.

Yet it is only a small step to go from this mentality of somewhat passively letting life happen, or feeling entitled or expecting it to and hoping for the best, to one in which you embrace all probabilities, including death.

Having either end of the human condition as a possibility makes life richer, the contrast sharper, and the good things taste all the sweeter when living and dying are both on the table. Optimism remains.

I can do as the old Latin phrase says and *memento mori*. I can *remember my death* and live accordingly. Having my end in sight, I ought to use the knowledge to live better. One can take the gamble of living, knowing that death is an inevitable outcome, possible at any moment, and live more purposefully as a result.

AS THE MATRIARCH OF THE family, Brenda is amazing. She carries on at her job in the assisted-living and nursing home, witnessing death with regularity while nursing her own grief with a cheerful spirit as she goes about her duties. I design a headstone with Brenda for Mark and the family. We put Jake's dates, Zach's birth date, and Baby Tiffany's dates on the back, each unmarried child accounted for. Whatever uncertainties might lie ahead, whoever is the next to go, ever-practical Brenda is prepared and is providing for her family as usual. She scrapes together small payments for us every month as she gets the funeral bill and the headstone paid off.

She always pulls up to the front door of the funeral home on the wrong side of the street (a perfect small-town move that I avail myself of often). As we have a window that looks out onto the road, I see her pull up, and run out to greet her. This drive-up arrangement we have always makes her chuckle about DuBore's commitment to service. But it's more than convenience; she is having some health troubles that make being on her feet too long difficult. She soldiers on at work and we're happy to give her a respite when she comes to do a drive-up drop-off.

And then one day, three years later, instead of Brenda pulling up to see me, I drive off to go get her.

Now Tasha, her daughter, finds herself the new head of her dwindling family.

Tasha finds the strength to plan yet another funeral with me. We've become friends through these sad and unexpected circumstances. In addition, Tasha is one of our mail carriers, so we see her a lot. She has joked about not wanting to see us again anytime soon. This time, though, there's less of a joke to it: she truly doesn't want to see us again. The weight of grief and responsibility is getting to her, and who can blame her? Now she's got her own young family to raise alongside her husband, and her brother Zach and his health struggles to look after.

Tasha had enough responsibility before all this and now she's got more dropped into her lap after burying her mother.

Surely, this should be the end of the story for Tasha. At least for a few decades.

But nine months later, Tasha finds herself the sole living member of her family. Zach has died following a bout of pneumonia.

We go to the graveside, and it is all too familiar. I don't offer empty words or try to placate Tasha. She's a realist, and damn if reality isn't unbearable. Zach's cousins bear his casket to the grave alongside his brother's, at the foot end of his mother's. His father is kitty-corner. Reverend Tom stands on Mark's grave as he now commits Zach to the earth. Ashes to ashes, dust to dust.

Tasha disappears.

She's crouched behind the hearse, alone, smoking a cigarette. What makeup was left on her face has made its way down her cheeks. A cousin approaches as I walk over (and I know her, too, as I buried her father the year prior). I give Tasha a hug and hold her very tight. Probably too tight and more closely than is professional. But it feels as if we've moved past professional at this point. We are simply two humans suffering together. That is the root of compassion, to suffer together.

Zach isn't my brother, but I see myself in him as much as I saw myself in Jake. Mark was the same age as my dad, and Brenda was always so kind and maternal to me. And Tasha is now a friend. We suffer together and it seems right. I can only offer her what I have—two arms to hold her up, along with the rest of my skills that have ushered her dead to where they will rest.

At least here, in Greenwood Cemetery, the family is at rest, reunited. Less one.

Tasha treads the grass on the way back to the grave. What was mortal of her family resides beneath our feet, but what was immortal of them surely resides within Tasha. She steels herself and looks down. She takes a breath, then joins her husband and sons, departing the cemetery, not feeling better, not knowing if the future will be bright, and surely not any stronger at this moment for outliving her family of origin.

The family who came into being through her parents' *memento vitae*—their optimism of love and creation—has now done what every family will eventually do: diminish one at a time until the last member remains. That it has happened so swiftly in Tasha's family is tragic.

Yet even here, in the tide of tragedy, what ebbs is followed by that which flows: Tasha has sons of her own who will likely bring her grandchildren. One accepts death and is practically forced to accept life along with it.

I TELL TASHA'S STORY HERE because there is so much death that has visited her family, and yet the optimism of life persists. We act and do this all the time, in sex and procreation. We live this optimism. Yet we don't always infuse the actual life of it all with the same spirit. I am admittedly unusual in the extent to which I have embraced death and come to fear little to nothing of it. The fear dissipates in the passion and curiosity and illumination I have found that accompany death in the shared moments along the way.

But what if I embraced living like I have already embraced

death, having no fears or anxiety about life, letting it happen, for good or ill, and embracing it with so much passion that it flavors every moment and influences all decisions, big and small? *Memento vitae.*

In my case, probably the most concrete way in which I can attempt to be at one with this idea is through my children. They find substantially more joy in high fives and knock-knock jokes than I do. To dip a chicken nugget in a sauce of their choosing is an exercise in adventure that I can only faintly remember. Some of that full embrace of life rubs off on me from time to time and I am grateful for it. I, too, get to play along and pretend that the broccoli florets on my plate are tiny trees and that I am more than a man, a giant at a dinner table of Homeric proportions. And yet the make-believe is reflective of a broader truth for me: I feel genuinely bigger when I live with the levity of a child. The hills and valleys of life seem much easier to traverse when I free myself from some of the constraints of adult preoccupation.

We all have things that make wonder in the world and, yes, sometimes those very things themselves snap us back to reality. It is the perpetual balancing act of being human, these flights of fancy and the stark dimensions of living.

A child begets wonder without meaning to. A child also requires more work than almost anything else. They nurture our souls as parents; but they also require an extraordinary amount of care. Half the time we know exactly what to do and unlock hidden parenting insights and powers within ourselves. The other half of the time we have no idea what to do and are bewildered, helpless.

It's hard to think of anything in life that doesn't come with some kind of trade-off. And so often, it seems, our preoccupation with these forces that snap us back to reality diminishes the potential for levity or joy. If we're consumed by all that can go wrong with children, we may just miss those perfect moments of sheer delight.

There will, sometimes, be abrupt changes (death) and challenges (life) that shake us and cause us to suffer deeply. But even were those changes to come, would we wish we filled the time leading up to them with anguish over their inevitable arrival?

As the poet Rumi writes, "The one who brought me here will have to take me home." However you believe we came into being, the action in and out of the world is much the same thing. The same kind of unstoppable force that brings us life is the same that takes us in death. By and large, the moments of our conception are ones of passion and vitality, and they come with optimism and a willingness to risk new uncertainty in exchange for new life. Though it is a tall order sometimes, letting that optimism balance the similarly unstoppable force of our end creates a greater harmony in the time that unfolds between our beginning and our end.

———•———

I ARRIVE AT THE NURSING home and Tasha is waiting for me. The time has now come for her grandmother.

"I said I didn't want to see you again," she tells me. I can't disagree. The cast of characters in this play is all too familiar. Sitting in her pajamas beside her grandmother's bed, Tasha makes a quip about looking like crap. I don't really notice. The fact that she came to bear witness to Delores Ann's last moments tells me what I need to know more than her disheveled hair and baggy T-shirt.

She still cares about life even in the face of death.

25

AN EPITAPH

Here Lies What Was Mortal of Paige Sweeney

THAT'S THE EPITAPH I'D CHOOSE for my wife's headstone were she to precede me in death. It tells a truth that's important to me, speaking of both body and soul and their division. It has a simple poetry to it that I find beautiful.

My wife knows about this and takes it in stride. She says the epitaph won't matter to her: she'll be dead. Married to an undertaker, you become nothing if not a little practical about the last things. Paige tells me she'd rather not have me use this epitaph and have her name carved into a slab of marble anytime soon, but she sees the practicality of thinking about what will happen when things change. Because things will always change.

And when that last change comes, the final one that

transitions us from living as we have been into something very much unknown (nothingness? everythingness? perfection?), there might be an anxiety for the world we leave behind and how we will be remembered. The big question of "what comes next" being unsolvable, these smaller unknowns may go without resolution.

If the unknowns plague you, you could throw your own funeral, like I did.

I had been ruminating on the idea for a few years. What if I attended my own funeral, à la Tom Sawyer? Would I have a casket there, closed, and watch it remotely as my friends paid their respects? Might I go one step further and lie in the casket, dressed in my wedding suit, as I have written down in my directives (it still fits and, worst-case, can be cut down the back to make it so in the event it no longer does)? How macabre would this get? I could ask my loved ones to give a eulogy and have them bear my casket out at the end. I could buy the attendees a meal and they could sit around and cry and laugh over me.

It's kind of a great shame that you don't get to enjoy your own funeral. Especially me—since it's literally the type of event I care about most and that colors my every day.

"Victor, you could actually do this, you know," Paige said.

"There's no way. And anyway, it's kind of tasteless, gathering at the funeral home and—"

"It doesn't have to be at the funeral home. And you don't need to be dead to get your friends together. I believe a gathering of friends is called a party."

And so, the foundation was laid for my funeral conclave.

IT'S TAKEN ME A YEAR to get the gumption to start lining this up. The trouble with telling someone an aspiration, even one as stupid as throwing your own funeral, is that once the thing is said aloud, one must go through with it, at least in my opinion. Otherwise, if you keep telling people your "someday" plans, the brain will trick itself into thinking the plan is done if repeated enough! You'll always be dreaming and never living that dream.

I buried Garrett's dad a few months ago. Vern had cancer and knew he was dying. He even came in and sat down with me, giving me a few papers detailing what he wanted, going so far as to hand me a copy of his obituary he wrote. His funeral was a strange thing. Just as happy and sad as most, with his gonzo sense of humor taking center stage at times. It also, dare I say, was kind of fun.

Some months after the funeral, Garrett's family and I finish walking around the Catholic cemetery looking at different species of granite for Vern and his (living) wife's shared headstone. It's nice to see the actual monuments and not just in a pamphlet or a photograph online. Seeing how the sun reflects off aggies, or the color granite takes on whether polished or honed, are the kind of details you get only when standing in front of the stone. We've discussed size and shape on our walkabout and are now huddled together, bantering. I immediately took to Garrett's family from the time we brought his father out of the house the night of his death. We find we can all easily partake in Vern's favorite pastime of making fools of both ourselves and each other.

While still gathered, I tell Garrett, whom I have now met a total of three times (at the place of death, at the funeral, and in this cemetery) that I have this idea of planning my own funeral, much like his dad did. Granted, mine has the twist that I want to have it while I'm alive. Garrett laughs and his sister teases it will be a "sausage fest." I tell her politely that, yes, there are no women allowed. A sausage fest it will be!

———•———

WALK THROUGH ANY PLACE WHERE the dead have lain buried for a few generations, and you'll find one thing in common with headstones that are anywhere from one hundred to two hundred years old. They may look old, but they don't look dated. An art deco monolith looks like it is from the 1930s, but there's a proportion to the size and line that speaks of the thoughtfulness of the person who designed it. A puritan gravestone with its childish carving of an hourglass or skull speaks to what the deceased believed about what was to come next. Even the ancient Nordic memorial rune stones have a sort of beauty that comes from the local material and the "realness" of the carvings.

The headstones of my region in the last forty years or so have been designed using clip art. A tractor, a loaf of bread, the image of a deer jumping (or lying down). It's been designed by a computer, carved by a machine, and it all feels a bit sterile. Rarely are words written on them apart from names and dates.

While it is of course a personal choice, I believe we've lost some of the sensibilities and craft that once made headstones draw out emotions or draw our minds upward to greater thoughts.

I think some of it is that we have a tendency in the modern day to reduce ourselves to the tasks of our lives. The work, the job, the label people knew us by for communal shorthand. And that's fine, but it seems too often where we stop. Instead of asking the "why" that informs what we did with our lives.

I recently came across a headstone erected for a local salesman of a certain household product we all have. The deceased was the longest-serving salesman in the nation for this brand. The logo for Stuff & Co. was sandblasted on Dennis's and his wife's headstone. His wife was a retired teacher, and her side of the stone had an apple on it. I knew Dennis. He was more than just a salesman for Stuff & Co. He believed in big things and fostered relationships that lasted decades. To boil his life down to selling various doodads was borderline irresponsible. The same goes for his wife. She formed young minds. Is an apple really all there is to tell that story?

I was told this was "what the family asked for." Maybe it was. But I would have loved to have helped them consider putting some thought into the stone that will forever stand over Dennis's grave.

One can always give a family exactly what they ask for in this business, but I believe it's far better to serve them with thoughtfulness, coaxing out of them the things that mattered.

The few epitaphs I usually see somehow aren't as evocative as those of the past. "Parents of . . ." doesn't count. I can dream up a headstone of noble simplicity that might look like this:

BOLTON

DENNIS R.	KAROL NÉE LISOWSKI
1926–2023	1928–DATE
STUFF & CO.'S LONGEST-SERVING SALESMAN	TEACHER AT ALVARADO SCHOOL
"IT WAS ALWAYS ABOUT THE PEOPLE"	"HE SHALL FIND HER SITTING AT HIS GATES," WIS. 6:14

We've now described their life's work, but also made clear that life was more than just doing a job. Karol's verse is from the Bible, and the "her" being described is Wisdom itself: a beautiful thing to try to impart to fourth graders. Dennis's quote is something he used to often say and how he approached his work and his life. The headstone is now personal and not simply stamped with a quick sort of personalization.

A good cemetery memorial, whether upright, flat, or somewhere in between, ought to engage the senses as well as the mind. I enjoy walking through cemeteries with old headstones, and as I do so, I try to keep my mind active by thinking about the people who inhabit the four-by-eight-foot plots of dirt beneath my feet. What were they like? What did they care most about? The cool thing about these near-century-old headstones is that they engage the senses as well as the mind.

Three of the five couples who lived in my house before me are buried in Warren's Greenwood Cemetery. I have stood on their graves and pondered what it was like when they trod the very floors that I walk every day. I left flowers at their graves this Memorial Day and will continue to do so to let them know I am thinking of them.

All memorials are made to be seen. It's rare these days that we make one to touch. This aspect of our experience of this world is forgotten when we render a 2D image into a 3D stone. The woman who built my house back in 1900, Mrs. Morck, has a headstone that is shell-rocked. This was a process by which huge, curved gouges were made in the granite. Her name is in a polished panel, but the rest of the stone is as craggy as a boulder. It's lovely. Rain catches in the indentations; a little moss grows on the north side, clinging to the rough-hewn stone. It has weathered over time, which makes it stand out in a good way among the rest of the highly polished and changeless stone tablets. Mrs. Morck's memorial is a thing made for solidity, to look at and see that it shall not be moved lightly. It is even a sort of stand-in for the indomitable woman herself. A woman who lived and died in Warren, Minnesota.

THIS PAST SUMMER, I OVERSAW the funeral of Noah, a little boy who had had health issues since birth, living only a few joyful years despite his parents' best attempts at getting him the right medical attention. I made arrangements for Noah's funeral, taking no payment, as we do with all children who pass through our doors. And while we do what we can, at times like these, even the best we can offer isn't nearly enough.

Four or five months later I sit down with Noah's dad, Henry, to talk about Noah's headstone. Henry works in the granite industry, and while he doesn't make headstones, he is interested in "feel." We talk about the tactile experience, Henry wanting his daughters to be able to touch their brother's memorial. As he speaks, I realize that in doing so, Noah's sisters will leave their handprints behind. Fresh flowers don't last very long. And a handprint is more personal, as no two are the same.

We start with a white stone, Sierra granite out of California. It is honed instead of polished. The years will show on the white as dirt blows in from the fields at harvesttime. It is no matter to his family, who pledge that they will clean it when they visit. I'm sympathetic. This is what we do, still, for my sister, Kate, who died thirty-six years ago.

I offer up some ideas about size and shape. It might be roughly his little boy's height. It will be semi-smooth, but not glossy. I order a beveled edge to soften the hard corners of stone that would seem out of place on a memorial for one so young and soft. Then we discuss Noah's epitaph. I throw a few out there. I want to tell the truth. I also want to grab the hearts of those who read it. They say a grief shared is a grief lessened. That we share it with the strangers of the future is no matter when losing a child.

I propose:

"Our boy of inquisitive mind and beautiful soul."

Henry and his wife, Vicky, offer this verse from the book of Proverbs:

"Lean not on your own understanding."

We use both.

Henry is a young father who has lost a son. He and Vicky don't know why it has happened to them any more than I do. Henry tells me that rather than ask the question "Why?" they just accept it. They don't lean on their own understanding, but upon each other and the beliefs that bind them together.

Henry's and Vicky's names are on the base of the stone as well. While fifty years might separate their eventual death dates from their son's, part of their story is now told in stone, uniting all three of them.

A FEW WEEKS AFTER I met with Garrett and his family, the time had come for me to make good on my own "funeral" gathering. I first thought I might have it in my backyard. We could set up tents and have a cookout, staying up late into the night, fueled by whiskey, beer, and tobacco. These last things being important, but by nature noisy, my lawyer buddy, Chris, offered me the use of his land. The same land on which I'd visited his future headstone. There was also a fire ring, an old hunting shack, and nobody to call in noise complaints in the sparse reaches of West Valley Township.

I don't need a hundred people at my funeral conclave gathering. What I do need is a pretext to gather, and "Come to my funeral" sounds like less fun than I think. The gathering becomes my thirty-second-and-a-half birthday party. I know plenty of people and am friendly with a lot of my acquaintances.

I figure if I am going to mix friends from all parts of my life, I need to curate the group and assemble this small crowd that will eulogize me at the day's end. I design elaborate invitations and address them in calligraphy to old friends (the oldest being from middle school) and newer friends (the newest is Garrett, whom I barely know). The invitation lists the invitees as follows:

> *Invitees include a skydiving instructor, a timber framer, a heretic submariner, a Catholic priest, two lawyers, a VCR repairman, a fluent Finnish speaker, a linguist/accountant, an app developer, a handsome funeral director, my brothers, and me.*

I also lay out what my guests ought to bring:

> *Please, no gifts.*
>   *Do bring:*
> - *Your swimsuit*
> - *Something to drink and share*
> - *Something to smoke and share*
> - *A game, if you like*
> - *A sleeping bag/blanket/whatever*
> - *A tent; or you may take a chance in the open*

Pretty low stakes, right? I then make up the not-an-itinerary. There's nothing on the agenda for our day in the country apart from swimming at a nearby state park, smoking chicken for dinner, and having a "roast or toast" eulogy before the night's end.

We'll see how the swim goes. I'm ready with my century-old, one-piece woolen swimsuit. Nothing better to break the ice with a group who doesn't know each other at all than by embracing my own foolishness and making everyone else take their shirts off but me. There are no secrets in death, just as there are no secrets in a tightly clinging wool bathing suit.

We meet at my house and carpool out to a nearby state park's very rustic water amenities. Awkward introductions are made, but soon dissolve into all-day inside jokes. Groups form and re-form as we splash in the swimming hole, wander Chris's woods, and pass around cans, bottles, and stories throughout the day. By nightfall, the eleven of us have eaten five whole chickens and are gathered shoulder to shoulder around the campfire.

I give everyone a birthday gift, Hobbit-style (where the birthday boy goes without and his guests leave with something), and offer a short speech. I don't have anything planned, but realize that I'd be committing a huge crime in this quasi-funerary solemnity if I didn't tell those assembled that I love them. "I love and appreciate you" has since become my regular sign-off with these men. I offer the floor for roasting and toasting, but my friends have taken the game seriously, and I'm touched. Even Garrett, who has taken a leap of faith and flown across the country from his home in Maryland for the party (telling his coworkers with raised eyebrows, "I'm going into the woods with my dad's mortician") has words of encouragement for this strange adventure he agreed to.

I remember all of what was said that evening and probably will until my final hours. Words of encouragement, of meeting many in the throes of grief, of being the "dad" of my college friend group, or the one zany enough to haul strangers to the woods and mortify them with my vintage swimwear. It was a beautiful thing. The goal of the event was achieved. Not so much to memorialize myself (although I certainly didn't mind that part), but rather the conclave achieved what funerals are meant to do—and what I hope my eventual funeral will do—bringing together a wide and unrelated swath of people for a common cause, making them merry, making them pause, and feeding their bodies and souls.

It's a blot on birthdays and other gatherings where, perhaps too often, we're not prompted to remind each other of why we're there—letting distractions or the comfort of small talk get in the way of connection and the savoring of it.

HAVING NOW HELD MY "FUNERAL," what would I want erected over my decaying flesh when my spirit ceases to animate it?

Give me a stone that weathers. Let the rain fall on it and make my name invisible in the damp. Let the dust blow in from the fields, sustenance that might otherwise go to feed barley or sugar beets, and let it find its way into the grooves of my death date and sit there sterile in my memory. Let the snow drift down and the slow expansion and contraction of ice-wedging have its way with the top, leaving it truly beaten from the elements. Let it be a reminder that all things decay, even this once bright and shining stone. Cut from the earth and worked on by human hands only to sit here for as long as it takes to work its way into dust, however slowly. To me, there is something serene in that.

If my name is illegible in a century, so be it. All those who will have known me will be old men and women by then. It's enough to know I was here. Probably a part of me still is. A femur head, some teeth, the handles of the casket that was carried by my friends to the grave. Part of me, too, is within the (now) old folks who knew me, and I even live a bit in the stories that are told of me, maybe thirdhand stories by this time, in which I am a faceless player known only by name, the timbre of my voice forgotten along with the rest. These things are all good enough. Let them stay.

My intended epitaph on the stone: While it is readable, let it be one that invokes a sense of mystery. Let it tell the truth but also leave the mourner or passerby to discover it themselves. I've done the hard work of dying, after all. They can do the work of deciphering the meaning.

He has seen much death and now he has conquered it.

What did he do to earn such an epitaph? Was he a doctor, saving the lives of many but not all? Was he given a fraction of a percentage to live and managed to live beyond expectation? Maybe he watched the world turn and the lives of men and women come and go in their time and that is all?

That's closer to the truth.

I saw the deceased on their departures. I washed and dressed that which was mortal with each person who came through my door. There's no image on the stone to tell you this. No sandblasted hearse or embalming machine to tell you of my trade and skill set. I like to think I was more than my occupation.

Look upon this and know that you, too, are more than your job. And whatever care I gave these bodies that lie beside me in the ground, the souls (or call them what you will) were beyond my purview. But I saw each day what was to become of me, the part of me that lies beneath your feet and the timeworn stone that you're reading by the light of a rising sun. It is early. If you're winding through the cemetery on a morning walk, know that you're a lot like me. And we share so much more in our humanity. You'll end up this way, too, or at least part of what makes you "you" will.

But my soul? That's the part that conquered death even if my body did not. It seems strange to say I "conquered" anything that I am now partaking in. Perhaps it's more accurate to say I became one with death and failed to escape it. But my soul was untouched. It remains yet, unbound to my moldering remains and bound up instead with all those things in which I believed, with Beauty, Truth, and Goodness—and, I hope, with the One who authored all of them in the first place.

26

THE CURSE

IT'S BEEN A ROUGH FEW weeks that have come, as always, unpredictably. Mike and I have done nearly 10 percent of our typical annual business in just twelve days. Four nights this week so far, I have come back in after the kids' bedtime and punched the clock from 9:30 p.m. to 1:00 a.m., doing paperwork, writing obituaries, and catching up on all the things left undone when the daylight hours are filled with death calls, embalmings, cremation deliveries, and, predominantly, funeral services.

It is a Thursday night at midnight, or should I say Friday morning. Mike and I are in the prep room, getting Daniel dressed, pulling plastic sleeves over the paper-thin skin of his ripped-up arms, sliding on his socks, and padding out his suit a little so he won't look so emaciated in the casket. As I am tying Daniel's tie, Mike and I are discussing what we might have done with our lives had we not chosen to burden ourselves with being in the death trade.

Mike was going to be an accountant. He finished a few semesters of college in the track before he found himself back at the family funeral home. In the late 1980s, he was working for his dad, Chuck, who has these days softened in a way Mike couldn't have anticipated. After butting heads with his dad, coupled with the stress of running the business, at one point Mike thought very seriously of changing professions. There was a position with an insurance agency that looked mighty tempting.

When things are particularly busy or stressful, I get tempted, too. My brother Bernard, a successful financial advisor, is always sure to let me know of openings where my skill set would serve me well: there's plenty of overlap in money management for a guy who enjoys getting to know the elderly. These openings are terribly appealing. I'd work less (and almost never at midnight), get paid more, and make a nice income living in the upper Midwest.

As we're lifting Daniel into his casket, Mike says (holding Daniel's feet while I've got his torso in my arms) he almost couldn't do anything else, though. I tell him I feel the same way.

"It's a curse, Victor. Once you start doing it, you grow to love it and nothing else looks as good."

"And the other opportunities are all so much more lucrative, right?" I say.

"Exactly. The guy who took that insurance job, he is already retired and living easy. And you can bet he never had to do this." Mike grunts as we lower Daniel into his casket and start to reposition him.

In a way, the job of being a small-town mortician is cursed.

He loves the job so much he's able to overlook the odd hours and the grisly scenes and the bother of asking for money to do it all. Even when he hates the job, he can't help but paradoxically want to do it more. Mike never planned to return to Warren and run the funeral home. It caught him in much the same way funeral service caught me, unexpectedly and with a tight hold. He bought his portion of the funeral home from Great-Uncle Rudy and has handled between eighty-five and a hundred deaths annually in the three and a half decades that have followed.

I think it might be a curse for me, too. I landed here, taking a job I thought would be temporary. Then a decade flew by. I feel I can't *not* do this. And I can't not do it in Warren. Buying my portion of the funeral home is on the horizon and, to be honest, I'm a little scared. Jumping ship to help old folks shuffle away assets with my brother never looked so good. But in spite of the fear of failure and concerns about how little I know about fully operating a business, Mike will be here to help. I can shuffle away elderly bodies easily enough, having done it for almost half my life. And my ignorance of the minutiae of accounts receivable or how caskets need to be priced to pay the bills, these are all things one can learn in due time.

The biggest hurdle I think I'll have is actually an odd one: nobody up here knows my last name.

When one is the only living "Victor" in the county (a true fact), the need for a further descriptor is almost unnecessary. Any further clarification is usually "Victor from the funeral home," or "Victor, the funeral director." My surname gives no tips to anyone, as it isn't a longtime local one. Were it a name that could place me in a family, or even a nearby town (like the French names in Argyle, or the Polish surnames in Florian), it might get some use.

I like being known by a mononym, and the sort of easy familiarity it brings is, I hope, comforting to families. But here's why it is a hurdle and something I've got to figure out: When I buy the funeral home, what will I call it?

Do I rebrand it as Victor's Place or Victor Funeral Home? Going by just my first name seems off somehow. Sven's Undercar Shop seems like a trustworthy place to get a repair (and it is). Victor's Undertaking seems . . . unprofessional. And Sweeney Funeral Home would just raise questions, as I still get asked my last name with regularity despite ten years of services here. Will there be a feeling of abandonment from those families I serve, thinking Mike sold out to some unknown entity? And if not felt as strongly as that, it still might take a few years to get people acclimated to a name they've never used. Maybe I just keep it as is?

I've floated the idea by Mike, and his advice surprised me. For a man whose family name has been above the door since the 1970s, he's not nostalgic about keeping it that way.

"If I could do it over again, I'd have changed the funeral home name to 'DuBore' right away."

(It was hyphenated with his great-uncle's surname for a few decades before "DuBore" was on its own.)

"Really?"

"Yeah, people were confused when we hyphenated, but by the end, they were calling it 'DuBore's' anyway. I'd say let her rip when you're ready."

I'm still unsure, but by the time it comes to buying in and operating the place, it will be settled. In any case, it is just a name, and a rose by any other name is just as sweet.

Maybe the same goes for the curse. As I am seemingly destined to remain here, despite other opportunities, maybe the curse is meant to be. Maybe by any other name we'd call it a blessing.

27

FRIENDS AMONG THE LIVING AND THE DEAD

THERE IS NO BETTER PLACE to end a thing than back at the beginning.

The narrow chasm between life and death allows us to straddle both the beginning and the end, to walk between these two and realize they are close. Are the final pages of a book that much different than the opening, which sets the story up? Both have to do with the delivery of expectation: before you dive in and after you've finished. I have plenty of books I think back on often, stories that happened to someone else that have in some way become my own, fictional or not. Let me tell you a few more stories and, as entrenched as these are in beginnings, they might give you a clue as to how we got here, at the end.

I have had three best friends in my life. Best friends come with the finest of beginnings, origin stories that you can look back on and see tiny slivers of what the friendship has now grown into. You think of the people you both were in the past, reflect on who the two of you are now, and realize that your friendship, as strong as it was even a few years ago, has become all that much stronger as time marches on. This growth is a type of magic that we all tap into with best-friendship.

That said, I don't believe you can have more than one best friend at a time. While I've had the advantage of having three best friends, the disadvantage is that two of them, as we say in obituaries, have "preceded me in death."

AS A YOUNG BOY, MY first best friend was my neighbor, Robby. His mother, Miss Carol, lived kitty-corner to us and was my day care provider. I'm no fool: Robby and I were best friends due to proximity. As we played during my day care hours and afterward, we were around each other constantly and were as close as two young buddies could be.

In general, I have rather vague memories of Robby. Much of what I remember is fueled by the few pictures I have of him. I remember Miss Carol more, but still somewhat hazily. But I do have very distinct memories of a certain time and place during that period.

The day Robby died.

I AM DROPPED OFF FOR day care at Miss Carol's as usual, jaywalking across the street to her house, hand in hand with my mom, who needs to get to work. We arrive and Miss Carol tells me that Robby hasn't woken up yet, but that I can run upstairs and wake him. He's had some exhausting days lately, having enjoyed Christmas with his father across town, who had custody of him for this year's holiday. But get him out of bed now, as there's a whole day ahead of you two.

I burst into his room and climb the ladder of his red metal bunk bed. He's got *Sesame Street* bedsheets and I pull them back to tap him on the shoulder: he's kind of cocooned in there. Robby doesn't flinch, roll over, or yawn. I try a few more times and call his name.

Giving up, I go back downstairs and tell Miss Carol he's not waking up.

Something changes. I remember the panic in her voice as she runs up the stairs, followed by my mom and then me. Some short time passes, and I hear a wail. My mind's eye can't recall this scene exactly, but the sound is one I have heard in my head ever since; a low, keening scream followed by a series of staccatoed nos. It is something of a blur after that. I remember Miss Carol sitting in the hall; I remember walking back home and looking over my shoulder as flashing lights pull up to the house. There's nothing else in my memory of the following days until his funeral, and even that is ambiguous.

I recall sitting in a funeral home chapel. Mom and Dad have brought me here and tell me it is okay, even if it is scary. Robby's casket is white. The inside is blue. He has his blanket and stuffed bear with him, the latter being something I think I'd like to take home with me. There are flowers and balloons and a pink overhead light providing him with a rosy glow.

And while Robby is gone from my sight after the funeral,

my parents assure me he is with me still, not truly gone, not just dead, but maybe more alive than before. I'm told I can talk to him still, and I do for as long as that novel idea has purchase on my developing mind.

In the months following Robby's funeral, Miss Carol moved away. Packing up her life and starting over, she sold most of her only child's things at a garage sale. I'm not sure if my parents made the connection when it came to the one thing they bought for our house. But it was hard to see how they could have overlooked it.

Mom and Dad came home with Robby's red metal bunk bed.

That my first big-boy bed was a literal deathbed isn't lost on me.

I suppose I accepted it like I accepted Robby's death: as something that just happens and isn't odder than anything else in a world I had barely experienced. This bunk bed was shared between my two brothers and me, all of us occupying lower and upper bunks in succession, into our teen years. Not that I think this was intentional on the part of my parents. It seems to me that they were rather practical about the whole situation: they simply needed a bed. Maybe that practicality took hold and continues to shape me? Whatever the case, I didn't realize the gravity of Robby's soul leaving his body behind in the top bunk until many years later. It must have been formative to me, but it had lain inside me as simply a story from my youth. This story had the weird O. Henrician twist of the deathbed, and that added a shock value when told. But I came to see this story more as something of value as I headed to mortuary school and began to usher the dead from the rooms in which their souls left their bodies. I realized that Robby's was the first bedside I attended. And all this at the tender age of three.

When you're a little kid, memories are fickle things. You see a photograph and convert it into something like a memory despite not having the actual "videotape" of it running in your head. Children's minds are easily swayed, and I wondered, as I began to think of Robby's finding as something more like a piece of an origin story, if what I remembered was true. Might it not be cobbled together from things my parents told me, mixed up with my own suppositions of what had happened that day?

The best way to find out was to check with the source.

I HAVE SEARCHED FOR MISS Carol on and off for the last decade. My folks stayed close with her for a while after she left town. Having lost their own daughter at a young age, there was a kinship between them that only parents who have lost children can possess. As the years passed and we moved away, too, they lost touch. I knew that she had gotten remarried. This is about all I had to go on.

It is 2023. I am working a visitation at the funeral home. In the time I have to myself in the office while a family service is being held, I begin to once again dig in. I find my childhood home on Google Maps and navigate across the street and over to her house. A search on the address tells me who has lived there in the past and claimed it as a residence. Miss Carol is on there. A few more rabbit holes give me the first lead I've found since the last time I picked up the trail, a possible married name—but there are a score of Carol Smiths in Michigan. I begin to sift through them, one by one. Within fifty miles of my childhood home I find a name match. This Carol is a professor at a Michigan university specializing in early childhood education. I write to her in an email.

Hello Miss Carol,

I'm not sure if I've got the right person, but I'm going to take a shot in the dark.

My name is Victor Sweeney, and I grew up in Royal Oak in the early nineties, kitty-corner to your home, and I was the same age as your son, Robby.

Assuming I have the right person, I wanted to reach out to you and let you know that I have never forgotten either of you.

Robby's death made such a big impact on me as a kid, along with the way my parents handled it.

I was there when his body was found that morning.

I've never forgotten that, either.

And the red metal bunk bed was bought by my folks right before you moved away; I slept on it my whole childhood.

Between that early experience, other deaths in the family, and just the twisting and turnings of life, I am now a funeral director and have been for a decade.

Anyway, I wanted to connect with you if this is you.

You're welcome to call me. I would love that.

And if I have the wrong Carol, please let me know and I'll continue my search.

Take care, and I look forward to hearing from you.

+Victor

I send the email off into the universe.

And while the family in the funeral chapel across the hall closes in prayer my phone buzzes.

I take the call.

A voice I haven't heard for thirty years begins to speak.

It is her.

I'm not sure how to describe it other than to say that I recognized Miss Carol's voice instantly. A gap of three decades and 90 percent of my life evaporated as I heard her speak. We hung up and video chatted. The terrible scream that had lain in my subconscious for years now had a "face" to go with it. Here it was, changed by the intervening years and yet somehow exactly as I knew it would be.

How does one begin a call like this? Thankfully a large part of my job is calling strangers to impart bad news or share in fresh grief. This is much the same. Ignoring whatever awkwardness there might be I launch in: "I don't know where to start, but I have never forgotten you. You are so familiar. I can't get over it. . . ."

"Victor, you are exactly what I hoped you'd be. Are you still precocious and use your middle name when introducing yourself? What have you been up to?"

I begin to tell her what has happened in the last thirty years and that my middle initial is used more frequently than the whole name.

Then I ask:

"May I tell you what I remember on the day Robby died? I don't know if it is all true, but I've worried for years it is something I've made up in my own head. . . ."

I then tell her the above remembrance.

And lo and behold. It matches.

Miss Carol fills me in on some details I didn't know. The neighbor, an ER doctor, rushed over to Robby's bedside before the ambulance showed up. Robby was taken to the hospital, pronounced dead, then autopsied. He was prone to seizures and had a fatal one in the night. And in her telling, his funeral had more details than I remembered, but the ones I did recall were accurate.

Robby is buried in Miss Carol's rural Michigan hometown

next to her parents. She didn't want him to be "alone" in a cemetery in Royal Oak, where she no longer lived. I understood.

We make plans to talk again, and we do.

I find out that she remarried and had another son. She went back to school and has been educating college students about child development, giving them both textbook learning and insights won from hard experience. She also had a heart transplant a few years back. Miss Carol is living with another woman's heart beating within her chest. Yet Robby is present in that heart as well.

Just as he is present in mine.

———•———

BEING ABLE TO CONFIRM THIS story was a gift, and maybe a testament to what imprints upon a child's mind when faced with tragedy. I was three, yet I had recurring memories of these things that many grown-ups would rather forget. Did I direct these awful things into something good? Something that informs what I now do every day? I don't know. Probably. If nothing else, the whole experience made me no stranger to death, this wild and terrible stalking thing that not one of us will escape. It might be that I've gleaned too much from it, but here I am.

The greater gift in all this wasn't the reassurance that my memories were true, but the connection I forged with Miss Carol. Finding that part of my beginning wasn't a lie was satisfying, but understanding that I now have an ending to the story is even better. I'm able to look ahead and see that, despite the chaotic memories of December 1993, both living major players, Miss Carol and I, walked away intact.

I sent her my family's Christmas card that year and will continue to do so. I call or text her from time to time. I'll be sure to get her one of the first copies of this book, initiated in some strange way from this shared experience, each of us drawing out the beginning of our life's work from the tragedy of Robby's early ending.

THEY SAY IN THE FUNERAL world that the two hardest kinds of deaths to deal with are the death of a child and a death by suicide. My experiences with my friends have included both. Having already devoted a chapter in this book to my next best friend's death and the fallout from that, I won't go into it again except to say again how hard it truly was. If my memories of Robby's death are disjointed, my memories of every moment following the initial call telling me that Alex died are crystal clear. I was reliving them one night as I lay in bed with my son.

My seven-year-old son, Arthur, despite being something of a wild man, has a very tender heart. In his natural, childish curiosity he asked me about Robby as we lay together reading in his bed. He knows I have two dead best friends—it is no secret. I told him all I could, not sparing details. He asked, "Did you know he was dead?" Thoughts of death have been on his mind the last few days, as I brought him along on a road trip to go retrieve a dead body. This is what undertaking dads do when stay-at-home mothers need a break. We didn't walk into a crime scene or even see a deathbed; rather, the two of us went to pick up a gentleman who was embalmed by another funeral home an hour or so away. It was not a scary experience, walking in and out of the funeral home together, Victor transferring Ralph to the cot and Arthur eating candy in the funeral director's office. And so, having tagged along on a safe introduction to the behind-the-scenes of the funeral world, Arthur has been thinking about death a lot.

As we continued our conversation, he asked about Alex. I became more emotional, even so many years later. I'm not sure if the wound will ever entirely close. It seems to reopen a little, not only in talking intimately about Alex but even when I experience a death of another whom I love. When my grandpa died, I wept openly. And while I was at it, I started crying about Alex all over again. This wound remains fresh, even as new feeble flesh tries to knit itself over when time begins to heal it once more, both a beginning and an end.

It seems proper to let my son witness these sorts of raw emotions, and even more the practicalities of death, lately. We're terribly frank around the dinner table: Who has died, or which visitation will I work this week to keep me absent from it? The boys will ask me how so-and-so died, and "Do I know them, Dad?" And even if they do, they know it'll be okay. In the midst of every seeming tragedy, there is always some good to grab hold of.

And in a lot of ways, these open wounds, these tragedies, these losses of my best friends, have built the beginning of my new best-friendship.

HAVING ARRIVED BACK IN THE office after lunch one day in October of 2019, I receive a message from my answering service in the form of an all-caps text: *JOHN ENGER—HAS QUESTIONS, WANTS TO MEET.*

I remember John well, having buried his father-in-law, Lloyd, the year prior. The message I took from my answering service in 2018 when Lloyd died wasn't a text but a phone call informing me that I was needed at a farm north of town.

It is the wee hours of the morning. It's awfully dark and I don't know where I'm going. I take a wrong turn and end up doubling back through the pitch-black roads to find nestled along a river the farmstead with lights on, unlike most other homes I pass along the way. These are the telltale signs of a death on hospice: porch lights on, front door open, faces turning anxiously to the window that provides the best vantage point to the road; each of these signals anticipating me, the man who shows up to chauffeur the dead away.

I arrive at the house and Lloyd's family is at his bedside, one that has been carved out for him on the main floor of the home, as most hospice bedrooms are. His wife, Julie, is there, as is his daughter, Emily—she's awake along with her toddler son. Lloyd's son, Ben, is sitting on the couch, and I've made certain in advance that Ben and John are around tonight. Being alone on the job, I always ask if there are stairs (here, they go into the garage and we will need to take him out that way) and if there will be some strong backs to help us down them. I can do a lot of things on my own or with little help, including wrestling bodies into body bags and carrying grandparents in my arms and down the hallway when the cot won't fit. But I never attempt stairs without some assistance. Were the son and son-in-law not here, I'd have called Mike to come and assist, but I don't usually drag him out of bed on his nights off unless it is desperate.

The light in the room is set on low and Lloyd looks jaundiced and yellow. The distinct smell of cancer (pancreatic, I find out later) lingers.

After I transfer Lloyd to the cot, clear the stairs, and roll the cot up the driveway, I urge it into the back of my van. The two men and I stand for a moment catching our breath. It is a beautiful night. While I was inside the house, the pitch-black sky shifted to a deep purple. The stars are out. It is breathtaking—so much so that the breaths we take in escape us again. For whatever reason, perhaps seized by the beauty and poetry of it all, I turn to John and Ben and tell them that what they've done tonight for their father, helping carry his body on its final journey, is a mitzvah: an act of kindness, of perfect charity. Unrepayable. Unrepeatable.

And with that, I say good night and drive slowly back into the fields and starlight.

Lloyd is a farmer and so his funeral is held in the evening, as he has died in the height of harvest season. The combines are still out in the fields, but I'm told it is easier to step away from duty when it is dark than in the rush of daylight. The church is crowded, and his daughter speaks eloquently of his carefree attitude. The family and I have gotten along easily enough throughout our time together, and I have enjoyed John and

Emily especially. We clicked well during our brief but rather intense "relationship."

Then a year later I get the text message:

JOHN ENGER—HAS QUESTIONS, WANTS TO MEET.

"Hey, John, good to hear from you. What can I do for you?"

"Hey, Victor. I'm a writer for Minnesota Public Radio and I want to do a story on you."

"Me?"

"Yeah. I can't stop thinking about everything with Lloyd. Especially the, what did you call it, 'mitzvah'? There's a story in there somewhere and I don't know exactly what it is yet, but can I just follow you around for the day? See what you do?"

"I guess so," I say with a shrug.

"Great! We'll figure out a time real soon."

Once we get a time set up, John arrives at my office. He's dressed in his usual getup of buckskin mukluks, worn-out jeans, and a black T-shirt. I almost don't recognize him despite the same large beard and pulled-back long hair. As intimate strangers, I invite him inside and we tour the funeral home. I might have walked him through the funeral arrangement process, but with John having sat in on a real one just last year, I instead go through everything that went down between the time I left the farmstead with Lloyd and his eventual burial. We talk about some of the things I've now written about in this book. Not knowing when the phone will ring, small-town politics, good bodies vs. bad ones, my dead best friends, and never denying charity. I'd have him come along on a death call if one were to occur, but we're left with a quiet day, and John joins me at home for lunch with my family. Not normally having an outlet for all these sorts of thoughts, I converse with him about all manner of things both closely and more peripherally related to funeral service. At the end of the workday, he drives home and leaves me to wonder what he'll come up with. There's little that makes a good news story in our day together, or so I thought.

When his radio spot about me hits the news, it makes a surprising splash. The article he wrote to accompany it gets picked up in the newspaper of the larger towns around me, and is carried by the Associated Press, and appears in syndicated newspapers nationwide. Robby makes his appearance in it, and John captures something that causes more than a few people to write me letters of encouragement or thanks.

A year later, *Wired* comes across the story John penned and contacts me to do a YouTube video answering "Dead Body Questions from Twitter." What I think will be a short video that maybe my parents and college classmates will see surpasses something like 14 million views in a matter of days.

And now, despite my best efforts of minding my own business at home and "creating content" in the form of a hundred funerals a year, this book is the product of those swirling thoughts in the background of a life's work around those no longer living.

All of this had its beginnings in a guy who saw something in me and the way I approached my work while mourning his recently deceased father-in-law.

John heard my story of Robby's death and the fresher story of Alex's and saw in these beginnings something of an ending as well. He may have had an inkling that it would end in a "viral video" and a book. He had no inkling that it would open to a new beginning in friendship. We now talk every day. Somehow or another the door was thrown open and I've found myself with a new best friend. Though I am well aware that being my best friend might come with the pall of death upon it, John seems to accept me picking his brain or giving him a passing thought of mine over a cup of coffee and a phone call most mornings. Just last week we were deep in discussion about a fella who died while having abdominal surgery. I express yet again my thoughts about that unusual overlap of holding in a man's guts while embalming on Saturday, only to hold his wife's hand during funeral arrangements on Monday. We talk about these grim realities and have bonded over much these last years, but the fact remains: my best friends' death rates have been catastrophic.

Hopefully it is a fluke. I have confidence that one can live a long and fruitful life while being my best friend. And if the worst happens?

I suppose John will do what every person throughout history has already done: die and see what happens next.

For as much as I say I walk between the living and the dead, it seems that maybe my position isn't special. Might it be that every one of us, in history and alive today, walks between the living and the dead? You and I are both very much alive. And someday we'll both be very much dead. And in the meantime, we'll watch loved ones come and go; watch them enter the world as inconvenient babies and leave this world as inconvenient old folks (if they're lucky). This dichotomy between life and death is still there: nothing we can do can make it go away. But knowing that these two ends of the spectrum are close to each other? That helps. And everything in between, maybe those things that fall into the narrow chasm between them, the one I like to think I bridge? Well, we might call everything that fills that narrow chasm "humanity" and rejoice in its comings and goings, all the while carrying on in our own less-profound daily comings and goings, knowing that the end is nigh.

And I'm here for it.

Waiting.

As yet, among the living.

AFTERWORD

THERE IS A PIOUS TRADITION of my devout Catholic forebears (pre–Vatican II) that, after the Funeral Mass is over, we pray for the person who is next to die among those congregated in the cemetery around the grave. That person could be anyone. Maybe it is the person to your left? Or maybe it is you?

Wherever you fall on the spectrum of spirituality, I offer this prayer to you, whoever you are: to that next person who reads this book and thereafter departs this life as we know it.

Your life has been a great gift to someone, and I hope that these words are a small but comforting gift to you.

May you find peace and pass over the narrow chasm, leaving life and greeting Death as one would a friend.

Your friend,
+Victor

ACKNOWLEDGMENTS

"I would maintain that thanks are the highest form of thought, and that gratitude is happiness doubled by wonder."

—G. K. Chesterton

I must first thank Paige, the Mort-Wife, who has labored long hours in our home while I've whittled away at this book late in the evenings, over lunch, and during the in-between times. The writing has been on the clock, ten to thirty minutes at a crack, so thank you to Mike and Chuck DuBore, who let me take over the desktop in the office and who have provided me with so much—both things I have written about and things unspoken. Thank you to John Enger, the one who prompted me to find a book agent and who has wasted countless hours on the phone with me as the thing took shape in my mind. To Sam Stutsman, who rescued the digital version of my manuscript from a sea of ones and zeroes an embarrassing number of times. To my book agent, Eric Lupfer, know that I cannot begin to express my appreciation for your tireless advocacy and for bearing me through the unknown. I'm grateful to Pam Cannon, my editor, who eased my frustrations in crossing from the funeral world to the author world. It has taken a certain kind of death (to self) to make the transition, and I think she bridged this particular narrow chasm with grace.

And a final thank-you to the many families I have served in my decade in Warren. Those who appear in this book, with only a few exceptions, are listed by their real names and in their real contexts; they know who they are. Each has given me a story worth telling. I only hope I have returned the favor in narrating their loved ones' lives and that to see a small fragment of them rendered in print is a balm to the soul.

ABOUT THE AUTHOR

VICTOR M. SWEENEY is a licensed mortician and funeral director in rural Minnesota. His videos, produced by *Wired*, have been seen by millions on YouTube, all while he carries on his day job, raises a handful of children with his wife, and gets the dead from point A to point B. Follow him on Instagram @Victor.M.Sweeney.